CONTROL + ALT + DELETE

A DICTIONARY OF CYBERSLANG

JONATHON KEATS

THE LYONS PRESS

GUILFORD, CONNECTICUT
AN IMPRINT OF THE GLOBE PEQUOT PRESS

The Lyons Press is an imprint of The Globe Pequot Press.

10 9 8 7 6 5 4 3 2 1

Printed in the United States of America

Library of Congress Cataloging-in-Publication Data

Keats, Jonathon.
  Control + alt + delete : a dictionary of cyberslang / Jonathon Keats.
      p. cm.
  ISBN 13: 978-1-59921-039-1
  ISBN 10: 1-59921-039-8
  1. Computers—Dictionaries. 2. Internet—Dictionaries. 3. English language—Slang—Dictionaries. I. Title. II. Title: Control plus alt plus delete.
  QA76.15.K434 2007
  004.03--dc22
                                        2007003226

INTRODUCTION

Language is a technology. Our first invention as a species, language is still our most powerful tool today, networking our societies and programming our machines.

Technology is a language. Most new words emerge from innovation because invention is how we change, fostering what we become.

Language defines technology. Technology defines language. And we go on creating astrolabes and laptops, aqueducts and internets, all introduced and preserved with words.

I am neither a linguist nor a technologist, but an amateur observer of language, living in San Francisco at the beginning of the twenty-first century. I write "Jargon Watch" for *Wired* magazine, noting new words as they appear: *blook* and *collabulary*, *microchunk* and *slivercast*. I jot these down in a leather-bound notebook with a fountain pen, and then turn on my Macintosh iBook to research them on the web. Using search engines such as Google and Technorati, I monitor the words in their natural habitat. And through collaborative research tools like Wikipedia, I examine how those words are collectively understood.

This dictionary takes "Jargon Watch" as a starting point, providing a broader and deeper view of technological language today than can be undertaken in a monthly magazine. Many of the words that I have chosen, such as *spreadsheet* and *email*, are now more than a decade old, and some, such as *algorithm*, have been variously used for many centuries. To most readers, many terms will be familiar, as they were to me before I set out to define them, yet time acts on language much as it acts on land: These words have accrued layers of meaning and folds of implication. To write about them today is to consider the ongoing significance of these technologies to our civilization.

Newer terms, such as *patching worm* and *enhancement divide*, fill out the story, reflecting how technologies have evolved, and how public attitude toward them has shifted. Likely, few of these neologisms will still be used in ten years' time. Machinery changes, as do metaphors. Unlike a website, which can continuously be refreshed, this book will age. The pages will fox and the binding will crack. Whatever we become, the text will remain a product of a specific time. Words introduced here will be preserved here.

More immediately, though, this book may be useful as a dictionary, defining terminology without which we simply cannot communicate in contemporary society. Concepts such as *biometrics* and *data mining* and *telepresence* are morally debatable, and the benefits of *artificial intelligence* and *ubiquitous computing* can be disputed as well, but not without the language to discuss them. We need to know the names and meanings of these phenomena in order to be responsible citizens, whether technophile or Luddite.

The reader will find that I am more the latter than the former. I acknowledge the value of technology, but I do not accept it for its own sake. My definitions express opinions. My research into everyday usage is inspired by the *Oxford English Dictionary*, but my attitude toward the research is in the tradition of Ambrose Bierce's *Devil's Dictionary* and Gustave Flaubert's

Dictionary of Received Ideas. I do this out of honesty: Living in the period that I'm chronicling, I have the privilege of seeing the culture up close, but not the luxury of neutrality. I am an amateur observer of language, living, inescapably, within the twenty-first century.

The title of this book is *Control + Alt + Delete*. It refers to the keyboard combination pressed to reboot a PC. The title is also a metaphor.

For readers who have never owned a computer, perhaps this dictionary will induce a reboot, an upgrade to the language of our time. But the title, like the book, is also directed at the digerati who, through this abecedary, might review the linguistic building blocks of modern-day complexity.

Our first invention as a species, and our foremost, language is the only technology powerful enough to question itself.

Jonathon Keats
December 2006

ABOUT THIS BOOK

Dictionaries are repetitive. Words are defined by other words, which are defined by others, until eventually—if the dictionary is complete—the cycle of definitions comes full-circle. This dictionary does not attempt to be complete, yet definitions do refer to terms defined elsewhere. Where this is the case, words have been marked in blue. The definition of cyberspace references virtual reality and telepresence. Definitions of hardware and software refer to one another. If this book is to be understood, it will not be read in lieu of technological engagement nor will it be used as an alphabetical training manual. It will be one piece of a life lived with technology—and technology will be one part of a life lived more broadly.

ACKNOWLEDGMENTS

I am deeply grateful to my editor at *Wired* magazine, Mark Robinson, and to editor-in-chief Chris Anderson, for the opportunity to write about language every month in Jargon Watch. And I'm heavily indebted to Lyons Press editor-in-chief Maureen Graney for suggesting and acquiring this book, and to Lyons Press assistant editor Jennifer Taber for skillfully and patiently seeing it to completion.

ALGORITHM (NOUN)

A set of instructions.

Cake recipes and computer programs are both algorithms, comprising abstract rules that can be followed to achieve practical results. Without algorithms, a computer will not run. With algorithms, a computer can be used not only to calculate taxes but also to trade on Wall Street or compose music. In both cases, the algorithms are reverse engineered: By observing the historical behavior of financial markets, or the musical compositions of Bach and Mozart, computer programmers can find patterns and formalize them as rules. These algorithms can then be used to predict future economic conditions, or to produce new music with different instrumental ingredients.

A-LIFE (NOUN)

Artificial life, as created on a computer or with robotics.

A-life simulates biological processes that can't be observed directly, such as evolution, allowing scientists to speed up living systems or run them in reverse. Researchers have simulated lifelike complexity of astonishing diversity, suggesting how our bodies and societies emerged from the primordial soup. From this, some deduce that the A-life models are themselves alive, claiming credit for the ultimate creative act, yet feeling not the slightest remorse for the carnage caused by turning the computer off at the end of the day.

AMBIENT (ADJECTIVE)

A passive display of information.

Ambient devices are nondisruptive, communicating with the user in ways that don't require direct attention, and may even be read subconsciously. While vibrating cell phones fall into this category, ubiquitous computing enthusiasts envision whole ambient environments in which subtle modulations in sound and lighting keep surgeons apprised of patients' vital signs or give traders a sense of stock market fluctuations. (The brightness of the room might be altered to signify trading volume, for instance, and different lighting colors might be associated with the performance of different stocks.) Ambient devices may even be incorporated into the decor: Engineers have built fountains that reflect changes in currency values by varying the heights of different geysers, a greater signifier of wealth than any font in Versailles.

ANALOG (ADJECTIVE)

A continuously variable signal or system.

While most computers are digital, human perception of the world is analog. Sensations are experienced as a continuum, from light to dark, say, or from loud to quiet. Digitizing those signals, by taking rigid measurements according to an arbitrary scale, makes them simpler to work with, yet loses subtlety. For this reason, analog electronics—such as in high-end stereo systems—have not gone the way of the adding machine. For artificial intelligence that emulates the human brain, old-school capacitors and resistors may even be state-of-the-art, an improvement over digital circuits.

ANALYTICAL ENGINE (NOUN)

The first general-purpose computer.

Designed in the 1830s by British inventor Charles Babbage, the machine required a steam engine to drive nearly one hundred feet of clockwork. While the Crown declined then to fund construction, programmers have recently emulated an analytical engine on a modern computer, where it works flawlessly. Together with Babbage's simpler difference engine—finally built in 1991 by the London Science Museum—the analytical engine operates today as a philosophical toy, a mechanism for speculation by technologists about how history would have been different had Silicon Valley been a suburb of Victorian London.

ANIME (NOUN)

pronounced *ahn-ee-MAY*

The Japanese word for "animation," *anime* is used by the rest of the world to refer specifically to animated Japanese films, videos, and TV shows.

A national art form as exalted as Italian opera, anime is, like Italian opera, stylistically distinctive yet diverse. Underlying the oversize eyes and exaggerated facial expressions, genres range from *sentai* (superhero) to *shojo* (little girl), *mecha* (giant robot) to *hentai* (pornography). More crucially, anime studios resist the corporate uniformity of Disney, often allowing each illustrator to approach the same characters with a different hand—meaning that the same character may have a different look from one film to the next. Fans may swap videos on laptops as often as they watch anime in movie theaters, and plots may tend toward the futuristic, but anime has less in common with *Shrek* than with *Aida*.

APP (NOUN)

A software **application, such as a** word processor **or a** web browser.

Apps give a computer everyday functionality, transforming an arcane calcu-
lating machine into a practical tool for doing business or communicating.
PCs are designed to be universal: Much as a food processor can slice or
dice or puree depending on the blade, a computer can crunch numbers or
parse sentences depending on the code. However, not all apps are written
for all computers. For instance, more graphic design software is compatible
with the Macintosh than with the Dell, because most designers used Macs
in the early days of desktop publishing. Those apps, as much as the slick
packaging, lend the Mac its fashionable reputation, though few who own a
Macintosh can distinguish between a point and a pica.

ARCHITECTURE (NOUN)

The structural organization of digital information.

Lacking the physical form of a public library or a file cabinet, the web can be disorienting for flesh-and-blood human beings. Information architects strive to make browsing intuitive, in the way that traditional architects try to make buildings easy to navigate. Good architecture depends on clearly labeled content and helpfully placed links, all guided by an ability to anticipate the behavior of an unprepared user. At present, the web as a whole resembles Mexico City or Istanbul, with well-designed houses haphazardly situated in municipal pandemonium. Proposals for a new semantic web, which would introduce global standards of organization, purport to elevate information architecture to the level of urban planning.

ARTIFICIAL INTELLIGENCE (AI) (NOUN)

The ability of a machine to reason like a human being.

Based on the assumptions that people are mechanistic, and that the advancement of technology is unlimited, AI seeks to mimic the behavior of the mind. This may be accomplished by emulating thought processes as understood by psychology (for instance, with decision trees), or by approximating the structure of the brain as modeled by neurology (using neural networks, for example). The success of artificial intelligence since the field was named in the '50s is as debatable as its premises: Researchers who believe the brain to be a massively parallel computer view every AI triumph (such as the victory of IBM's Deep Blue in a 1997 match against chess grandmaster Garry Kasparov) as evidence that machine consciousness is inevitable, while those who see the mind as something more than three pounds of wetware attribute every AI accomplishment to something other than intelligence proper. Oblivious to the argument in philosophy departments, AI has planned military maneuvers, and neural networks routinely detect credit card fraud using data mining skills beyond human capabilities—suggesting that perhaps we should not consider ourselves the benchmark of intelligence.

AUCTION (NOUN)

An online marketplace that caters to people who wish to buy and sell items, often at bargain prices.

With an international clientele and a world of items to buy and sell, companies such as eBay, Amazon, Yahoo!, and Overstock.com have made the online auction one of the foremost sources of trade and recreation on the internet. Unlike most internet businesses (such as online pet supply companies or grocery stores), online auctioneers never needed to justify their existence: From the moment that eBay founder Pierre Omidyar sold his first item—a broken laser pointer purchased for $13.83 by a self-described broken-laser-pointer collector—the explosive potential of an expansive marketplace was more than economic theory. Billions of dollars later, the web has seen everything from a submarine to a cornflake go to the highest bidder. While the former, sold by a New England town, might otherwise never have found an interested collector, the latter, auctioned by a Coventry University student, reached its winning £1.20 bid through the sheer pleasure of competition. Comparisons to online gambling by cyber-puritans are extreme, yet both industries, lucrative long before the internet came along, have always essentially been in the business of entertainment.

AVATAR [NOUN]

A digital representation of a participant in an online environment.

Avatars in computer games may be stock icons as generic as the player tokens in Monopoly. At the opposite extreme, in virtual worlds such as Second Life, people who spend the majority of their social life on the internet may concentrate on their avatar's graphic attributes more than on their own physical appearance, making magnificent efforts to look distinctive. Those who can't manipulate the graphics software themselves often hire professional designers whose rates rival those of a personal trainer, yet who can perform operations that a personal trainer cannot, customizing build completely to owner specifications, and, for a price—sometimes more than a thousand dollars—adding highly desired sex organs.

BACK DOOR (NOUN)

A secret passageway into a computer system.

Often installed by computer programmers for ease of access, back doors can be exploited by hackers seeking to break in unnoticed to steal information or impress their friends. In the movie *WarGames*, a breached back door famously puts the world on the brink of thermonuclear war. More commonplace, though slightly less dramatic, is the use of back doors by spammers, who worm their way into vulnerable systems, reprogramming computers to send junk email 24/7 about penis enlargement.

BANDWIDTH (NOUN)

A technical factor in the rate of data transmission over the internet, mathematically defined by the frequency range of a signal as measured in hertz.

Bandwidth is used by most people, unfamiliar with the details yet taken by the authoritative sound of its jargon, to signify the speed with which they can send email or navigate the web. Some even apply the term to themselves, referring to their attention span as mental bandwidth—which is often inversely proportional to the so-called bandwidth of their internet connection.

BANNER (NOUN)

An ad on a web page.

The billboards of the information superhighway, banners advertise everything from fast-food chains to internet dating services, all in an attempt to help subsidize the free content of many websites. Banners are named for their prominent positioning across the top of web pages that advertisers believe will be visited by their target audience. For example, a luxury resort might buy banner ad placement in the travel section of an online newspaper, paying a ten-cent premium each time a reader clicks through to the advertiser's website. Of course, few people will admit to succumbing to these banner ads, just as few will admit that they choose their brand of toothpaste based on TV advertising. Yet the number of clickthroughs is substantial enough to support much of the material that makes the web interesting, proving that commercialization is not necessarily opposed to creativity.

BENCHMARK (NOUN)

A standard for comparing the performance of different electronic devices.

Because of the diversity of components and the complexity of their inter-action, the most accurate way to determine whether one computer works better than another for a given purpose is to run the same software on both. For this purpose, special software has been developed. However, in an attempt to make their brand stand out in stores, manufacturers often spend more time optimizing their benchmark testing procedures than improving their hardware, touting results of no relevance to real-world users—a practice called *benchmarketing* by competitors unable to cheat as effectively.

BETA (NOUN)

pronounced *BAY-ta*

The programming stage in which new software is tested by paid professionals or the general public prior to official release.

Corporate emphasis on "extras," such as fancy graphics useful only for generating marketing copy, ensures that software emerging from alpha-stage programming won't run properly. Beta testing is intended to tell developers what needs fixing without risk of widespread embarrassment or expensive patching. But the beta stage, like adolescence, is now often prolonged throughout the life of the application, especially in the case of open source software, which is always in development. Even software that leaves beta generally doesn't go into general release without problems—leading some paying customers to call themselves, ruefully referring to the next letter in the Greek alphabet, *gamma testers*.

BIOMETRICS (NOUN)

Personal identification through the measurement of physical attributes such as fingerprint patterns.

Originally developed to track criminals, biometrics now augments ID cards in airports and verifies tickets at Disney World. While the ease of collecting and applying biometric data, with digital imaging and searchable databases, has made scanning of hand and retina technically feasible, fears of identity theft have made biometrics socially acceptable—another instance in which we voluntarily accept criminal treatment for ourselves.

BIOMIMESIS (NOUN)

Culling innovations from evolution, biomimesis looks to nature for technological inspiration.

Velcro is based on the way that burrs snag fur, for instance, and radar applies the principle of echolocation long ago mastered by bats. Despite the success of these inventions, biomimesis was rare in the industrial age, when the aim of technology was to supersede nature. The recognition that human survival depends on the planetary ecosystem—and that the web of life supporting our species is too complex to comprehend—has led technologists to consider machines that operate more in harmony with nature. Biomimetic systems such as photosynthetic power plants based on the structure of trees may be not only smarter than anything we could have imagined, but also better for us than we can fathom.

BIT (NOUN)

A binary digit, either a 1 or a 0, the basic unit of data storage on a computer.

While one bit in isolation is essentially meaningless, strings of bits, in eight-bit units called bytes, can contain the text of an email message, for instance, or the set of instructions that tells a computer how to send that email over the internet. In fact, the size of any file or application can be expressed in bits or bytes. Most text and image files are at least several kilobytes in size, most applications are many megabytes, practically all hard drives can store gigabytes of data, and the complete contents of the National Archives, currently undergoing digitization, is expected to be nearly an exabyte (1,152,921,504,606,846,976 bytes), though storing large amounts of data is less challenging than making sense of it.

BLOG (NOUN)

pronounced bLAHg

A free personal online journal, frequently updated, often without editing, concerning subjects ranging from the international regulation of atomic weapons to the inner turmoil of suburban teens.

An abbreviated form of the already obsolete word *weblog*, the term *blog* has proven nearly as adaptable as the technology, with a blogosphere of subgenres, including the photoblog, the moblog (a blog to be read on the mobile phone or PDA), and the vlog (a video blog). All are characterized by ADD-friendly brevity, which perhaps explains the medium's explosive popularity—growing from several dozen sites in the mid-'90s to more than fifty million today—and the extensive political power of some practitioners: Responsible for the resignation of Senate Majority Leader Trent Lott in 2002, the political blog, or plog, is arguably more significant in soundbite-sensitive policy making than the newspaper editorial, and the plog convention known as YearlyKos has even become a destination for wonkish presidential hopefuls.

BLOOK (NOUN)

pronounced bLUHk

Taking inspiration from the blog, a blook is a book without paper or ink, published online and read on-screen.

Alternatively, taking content from the blog, the blook is a book initially posted in online installments, and subsequently published between cardboard covers. While the former is an eco-friendly invitation to eyestrain, the latter gives authors the opportunity to build a readership for a book before it exists. Reader comments may also be incorporated, a means of crowdsourcing content that often adds layers of unexpected research and, in the best cases, can inspire writing of Talmudic complexity. Blooks such as *Julie & Julia* by Julie Powell have had great success as printed books. A Lulu Blooker Prize, based punningly on Great Britain's Man Booker Prize, has been established to recognize online efforts with the greatest potential—and also to promote Lulu.com, leading purveyor of print-on-demand blooks.

BOOKMARK (NOUN)

Preserving URLs for future reference, bookmarks maintained on a web browser provide an easy means to revisit sites of personal interest.

In this respect, they resemble the ribbons or cards used to index important passages in books since medieval times. The crucial difference is in the web itself, changing constantly and accessible to everyone simultaneously. Social bookmarking, which makes participants' bookmarks available to anybody with an internet connection, transforms a personal convenience into a public service: Users sharing bookmarks have created an alternative to the machine logic of search engines, providing an individual read on the world's largest library.

BOT (NOUN)

An internet robot, programmed to perform online tasks automatically.

While steel-and-silicon robotics remains primitive—most machines still can't negotiate a staircase—bots are often more efficient than humans, unfettered by slippery mouse pads and sticky keyboards. (Bots are indigenous to the internet, whereas we can only visit.) Some bots crawl the web, mapping cyberspace for search engines. Others interact more directly with the public, working as virtual customer service reps for companies by responding to instant messages with stock answers to standard questions. Yet others are more sinister, sending spam all day long from computers on which hackers have illicitly installed them, taking remote commands from their masters as part of vast underground *botnets*. With numbers increasing, and spam becoming ubiquitous, bots may one day have the internet entirely to themselves.

BROADBAND (NOUN)

Any faster-than-dial-up internet connection, often using telephone lines or wi-fi, but occasionally, in rural areas and third-world countries, resorting to access by satellite.

Given that nearly all web content is posted by broadband users who haven't encountered dial-up since the last millennium, most sites assume that broadband is universal, flaunting elaborate visuals that would make any modem choke. While connection rates continue to increase, and will get a significant boost when technology is developed to send signals through power lines, the alternate name for broadband, *high-speed internet*, is no more accurate today than it was five years ago, since the content being delivered is so much more extensive than it was half a decade ago: The growing complexity of multimedia, especially streaming video, can drive Luddites to reach for a book.

BROWSER (NOUN)

An application for viewing content on the web.

Because web pages are written in one of several standard computer languages, a browser can read any URL and display any website. This universality, together with universal indexing by search engines, is what prevents the web from becoming a virtual Tower of Babel: While nobody can possibly apprehend everything in cyberspace, all is accessible to anyone. The web has no regionality. To encourage exploration, most browsers include a search engine window, as well as tools for bookmarking pages of interest. In fact, little differs among major browsers, such as Microsoft's Internet Explorer and Mozilla's Firefox, despite fierce competition between the two companies. The requirements of universality leave little room for individuality.

BUG (NOUN)

A minor glitch in computer software **or** hardware**, which often results in major problems for the user or owner.**

According to legend, the first bug to cause system malfunction was a moth caught in one of the relays of a Mark II computer at Harvard shortly after World War II. While the term predates this act of insectine sabotage by well over half a century, the popularity of the story suggests the border-line paranoia of many engineers, loath to accept that the bugs in their code or circuits are of their own making. Their sense of victimization is under-standable, as bugs are generally very difficult to detect and all but impos-sible to predict, and debugging a program during beta testing may be more time consuming than writing the code in the first place. Moreover, the price of missing a single bug may be catastrophic, crashing airplanes and power grids—as happened when fifty million Americans and Canadians lost power on August 14, 2003.

CAD (NOUN)

An acronym for "computer-aided design" or "computer-assisted design."

Originally the architectural equivalent of a word processor, CAD software has evolved over the past half century to become the central processing unit of the built world. In CAD, an architect or engineer can lay out a complex, three-dimensional structure—a skyscraper, say, or an engine—in such a way that the drawn components physically interrelate: Move the rectangle representing a steel beam and the position of the cylinders representing bolts at either end will be repositioned with it. Once given information about the materials to be used, and environmental conditions, the computer can simulate how the structure will fare on the ground, and *CAM* (computer-aided manufacturing) can even partly build it using industrial robotics. In some software, structural elements are maneuvered graphically with a mouse, while other systems, often called parametric, are manipulated by changing the values in mathematical formulae. However, all depend on the user's ability to work conceptually, designing in terms of how components will function together rather than how they appear. As a result, architecture has become largely a form of engineering, functional and pragmatic, with only masters such as Frank Gehry capable of transforming mechanical properties into poetry on the skyline.

CASUAL GAME (NOUN)

A computer game with rules simple enough to attract casual play by people who wouldn't be caught dead in a Dungeons & Dragons lair.

Casual games are often adaptations of popular board games such as checkers, or card games such as blackjack, programmed for play on a PC or PDA. Hard-core gamers mock the 2-D graphics and scorn players' lack of seriousness. In the latter respect, they are in agreement with employers, who have lost countless man-hours of work to casual procrastination in the years since Microsoft first playfully included computer solitaire free with the Windows operating system.

CD  (NOUN)

A compact disc.

Originally developed by the music industry as an alternative to records and cassettes, the CD has also become the standard medium for distributing software and storing data. Not all CDs are the same, however. The CD-ROM is mass-produced and permanent, while the CD-R can be "burned" with data, storing files on a computer. While less durable than CD-ROMs, CD-Rs will preserve that data for more than a hundred years, according to the accelerated-aging tests of manufacturers. Of course, they don't mention that the disc will be meaningless without a CD drive, and that the electronics in computer hardware seldom survive for more than a couple of decades—eventually rendering CDs as useless as eight-tracks are today.

CHAT ROOM (NOUN)

An online forum for realtime conversation between people with common interests yet no physical connection.

There are chat rooms for preadolescent girls who like to trade clothing tips for Barbie dolls and chat rooms for young professionals who want to share stock tips and chat rooms for retirees eager to talk about their RV excursions. Chat rooms are often compared to cocktail parties, where people converge to socialize and to make new acquaintances. To an extent, this is accurate: Netiquette, passively enforced by all participants, generally controls behavior as strictly as would social mores at a mixer. (*Flooding*, or typing too much, will be collectively shunned, for instance, and only certain environments are deemed appropriate for cybersex hookups.) However, the fact that most chat rooms resemble computer games, often with 3-D avatars representing participants, gives them a distinctly unreal quality, in which chat becomes a form of self-conscious role-playing—a quality that has increasingly spilled offline into real-life conversation.

CHIPTUNE (NOUN)

Electronic music generated by computer chips.

The first chiptunes, basic sound effects for '80s video games, were created simply because recorded music used more memory than early computers had available. Only after computers became powerful enough to trounce the New York Philharmonic for sound fidelity did chiptune beeps and beats attract real musical interest. Computer-driven *bitpop* can evoke youthful arcade days for nostalgic Gen Xers as reliably as the strum of an acoustic guitar can transport boomers back to Woodstock. And *circuit bending*, the art of selectively short-circuiting old game consoles to create strange new soundscapes, makes the theremin seem as traditional an instrument as a Steinway grand.

CITIZEN JOURNALISM (NOUN)

Do-it-yourself news reporting, aggregated and published on the web.

Citizen journalism combines the stridency of grassroots political movements with the amateurishness of personal blogs, challenging the mainstream media (*msm* in citizen-journalist jargon) on grounds of bias and elitism. Given public disdain for the press, citizen journalists have gained considerable traction in the past several years. Politicians, traditional enemies of the media, have been especially keen to embrace citizen journalists, providing credentials to conventions and interview access. As a result, citizen journalism has recently had a significant impact, especially in South Korea, where the forty thousand citizen journalists collaborating on OhmyNews helped elect Roh Moo-hyun to the presidency—a public display of power if not objectivity. At their worst, citizen journalists have the collective instinct of a mob. At their best, they serve as individual eyewitnesses, often with cell phone cameras in hand, covering more ground than would be feasible for any news organization. In another era, less prone to hype, they might simply be termed whistleblowers.

CLICKPRINT [NOUN]

A unique online fingerprint based on web browsing **behavior.**

Measured in terms of time spent on a website and number of web pages viewed, a clickprint can help an e-company identify return customers with 87 percent reliability after as few as seven visits, and with nearly 100 percent accuracy after fifty sessions—potentially useful information for target marketing. Clickprints furthermore provide an effective means of combating online fraud when used to verify credit card information—but they also can provide a powerful data mining technique for law enforcement personnel to abuse in their never-ending quest to find activity suspicious.

CLIPART (NOUN)

Digital images prepackaged for desktop publishing.

Tending toward the cartoonish, clipart often illustrates family newsletters and pizza parlor menus, though professional graphic designers may use it ironically in place of creativity. Many clipart images predate computers, originating in the paste-up era, when the pictures were physically clipped from books and glued down on illustration boards for photomechanical reproduction. Scanned and compiled in massive libraries often comprising a million pictures or more, clipart images of every conceivable animal, vegetable, or mineral can now be found for pennies on the web.

CLONE (NOUN)

Mimicking popular name-brand hardware **or** software **in all but cost, clones are to technology what generic drugs are to medicine.**

The word was first applied to computers manufactured by companies such as Compaq, which offered machines compatible with the IBM in the '80s: While the IBM name initially gave PCs widespread credibility (based on Big Blue's long-standing business reputation), clones introduced affordability and added functionality, allowing the PC to outgrow its infancy. Despite the often derogatory use of the term, more recent cloning of hardware and software, including the UNIX operating system, has likewise prevented innovation from suffocating in the tight grip of a single corporation—making the market more vibrant and lucrative for everyone. Working at the margins of patent law, relying on dark arts such as reverse engineering, cloning keeps invention honest by finding alternate non-infringing solutions to engineering problems. Often devilishly clever in their own right, clones are unexpected drivers of creativity, inspiring improvements in the machines they set out to copy.

CODE (NOUN)

The text of a computer program, code tells a computer what to do and how to do it.

Code is the linguistic common ground between human and machine. While programmers code in many different computer languages, including Java and C++, certain stylistic traits, such as clarity and simplicity, are universally esteemed. Such qualities make little difference from the standpoint of the computer, which reduces everything to strings of numbers, yet are essential for communication between coders, who often must struggle together to comprehend how their code is being interpreted or why it isn't being understood. The perfect logic of computers is confounding even to the most rational of engineers. For this reason, programmers will speak of writing "some code" rather than "a code," the implication being that there will always be more coding to do in the future.

COLLABULARY (NOUN)

pronounced *call-AB-yoo-lay-ree*

A collaborative vocabulary for tagging web **content, such as** digital **photography, so that others can find it using a** search engine.

Like the folksonomies used on social bookmarking sites such as del.icio.us, collabularies are generated by the community, with individual users introducing descriptive terms, such as *tallest* and *highest* for Mount Everest. Unlike folksonomies, they're automatically vetted for consistency by computers, extracting the wisdom of crowds from the cacophony. (For instance, the computer might determine that *tallest* and *highest* are inter-changeable terms for mountains.) In a sense, collabularies emulate the natural evolution of language, the give-and-take between casual speakers and official dictionaries that keeps expression current while preserving a common tongue.

COMPATIBILITY (NOUN)

Technological harmony.

Systems are compatible if they work together, regardless of whether they were built to fit. For instance, the ability of a new computer to run old software, or of new software to run on an old computer, is a matter of compatibility. The initiative can occur on either side: Backward compatibility allows a newer system to emulate an older version, like an urban hipster wearing overalls to visit farm country, while forward compatibility makes a system indifferent to anything it doesn't recognize, like a farmer who ignores the hipster's three-hundred-dollar sneakers.

COMPRESSION (NOUN)

Reduction of digital file size for transfer or storage.

Because digital audio and video equipment often records more detail than is perceptible to human audiences, file sizes can be decreased by selectively discarding what won't be missed. Savings to computer memory may be substantial, and compressed files in familiar formats such as MP3 are ideal for rapid distribution over the internet, yet the bits lost through the compression process can never be recovered, and the mere knowledge that they're gone can haunt music and film aficionados like a phantom limb. Lossless compression, which finds patterns in data and eliminates repetitions, avoids such problems, and has worked wonders for such rousing songs as "100 Bottles of Beer on the Wall."

COMPUTER GAME (NOUN)

An interactive digital amusement.

From shoot-em-ups to simulators to MUDs, games elevate computers above mere utility by making them entertaining. Alternatively, games may be seen as the downfall of productivity in the digital age, making PCs into machines for on-the-job procrastination. Games develop observational skills, hone reflexes, and train people to engage with the world; games foster a passive society, able to live only vicariously; games are the cause of modern aggression, encouraging violence, providing target practice; games build empathy by allowing players to experience the fate of their online avatars. . . . The reason there are so many conflicting opinions is that there are so many different genres of games, and so many different ways of playing them. An adventure story spun out in 3-D on the internet with a community of thousands is not the same as a puzzle thumbed at by a bored commuter on a cell phone. A game is defined, in the act, by the players.

COMPUTER SCIENCE (NOUN)

The study of computation, an academic discipline that shares interests with fields including mathematics, linguistics, neuroscience, and philosophy.

Computers are the experimental platform of computer science, much as fruit flies are a test bed of genetics: Attempts at endowing a machine with artificial intelligence, for instance, test theories about the human brain, as well as language and logic. And just as genetics has led to practical advances in medicine, computer science has spawned countless technologies, including the PC and the world wide web. As a result, hardware and software engineering are also often categorized as computer science in classrooms and conference halls. Astute computer scientists have responded by researching the by-products of computer engineering in new fields such as ludology—the narrative study of video games.

CONSOLE (NOUN)

A computer designed exclusively for video game play.

The sports cars of home electronics, consoles such as the Microsoft Xbox and the Sony PlayStation feature designer looks and high performance, with specialized controls built for hairpin precision in demanding situations. Of course, like the sports car, the console is all but useless for getting work done: There's no keyboard, for instance, and the processing power is optimized for the graphic requirements of virtual gunfights and car chases. Nevertheless, some scientists claim that this play is essential preparation for children growing up in a graphically driven interactive age, and games are increasingly popular for preparing soldiers for war. Even if the revolution is not televised, it may well be played out with maneuvers learned on Xbox.

CONTROL + ALT + DELETE (NOUN OR EXCLAMATION)

The title of this book. Also the name of a Polish alternative rock band, an electronic music zine, and a web comic—all inspired by the keyboard command for restarting a recalcitrant PC without unplugging it.

In the early '80s, an IBM engineer named David Bradley selected the control, alt, and delete keys, all of which must be pressed down at once, for internal use by programmers as a quick-and-dirty escape from malfunctioning software. Yet as companies such as Microsoft began releasing buggy applications, sacrificing quality in favor of market share, average users learned to reboot their own computers using control+alt+delete, dubbing it "the three-fingered salute." (As Bradley once said, "I may have invented control+alt+delete, but Bill Gates made it famous.") The term is now more generally associated with anything undertaken anew, as a slogan for initiatives ranging from self-improvement to political reform.

COOKIE (NOUN)

Cookies allow websites to identify return visitors, adjusting content to reflect previous visits, picking up crumbs from past interactions.

For instance, a weather information site will automatically select maps of regions viewed before, and an online shopping site will call up former purchases, and sometimes make suggestions based on detected patterns: Purchase a book by Judith Krantz on Amazon and you can count on being hustled to buy the latest Danielle Steele title within a few weeks. The server isn't psychic, but simply relies on a unique sequence of numbers stored on the user's computer, and surrendered on the next visit.

COPYLEFT (NOUN OR VERB)

Subverting copyright law, a copyleft license ensures the free and shared use of intellectual property in perpetuity.

Copyleft-licensed software, most notably the GNU operating system, may be modified and distributed without limitation, provided that any software derived from it is issued under an equivalent copyleft license. In this way, programmers can create nonproprietary alternatives to the regulated products of companies such as Microsoft without risk of having their own software restrictively exploited by others. Copylefting applies courtroom decorum to hacker anarchism, appealing to people who believe that intellectual property protection—originally enacted to motivate invention—actually stifles creativity by discouraging voluntary, unstructured collaboration.

COSPLAY (NOUN)

pronounced *COSS-play*

Costume play.

For the most dedicated fans of computer games, merely maneuvering avatars on screen is not enough. Cosplayers also dress up as favorite game characters. In Japan and the United States, many hours of work go into preparation for conventions where cosplayers show off and compete. The fanciful forms of animated robots and aliens are faithfully replicated in cardboard and spray paint. More difficult to imitate, though, are anime-inspired humanoid characters, whose supermodel proportions are not easily applied to the average gamer's unshapely body.

CROWDSOURCING (NOUN)

Outsourcing product innovation to customers, crowdsourcing provides companies with a cheap and quirky alternative to traditional research and development.

At the core of crowdsourcing is the internet, which businesses use to locate hobbyists with specialized interests ranging from particle physics to furniture making. Those amateurs are enlisted to solve specific engineering problems for a small fee, or invited to submit product ideas to design competitions over which hundreds or thousands of fellow customers preside as judges. The former strategy has been used successfully by large corporations such as Procter & Gamble, which posts R&D challenges to a crowdsourcing clearinghouse called InnoCentive, where nearly a hundred thousand "solvers" search for projects to fill their spare time. The latter approach to crowdsourcing is more often used by smaller companies, including the Japanese furniture retailer MUJI, which allows people to submit design ideas to the corporate website, manufacturing only those that elicit enthusiasm from potential buyers. For businesses, crowdsourcing is foolproof. And for the crowdsourcing workforce, the validation of a hobby by a large company is something to blog about.

CULTURE JAMMING (NOUN)

Repurposing mainstream media as a channel for political activism.

For decades, billboards have been illicitly altered to deliver anti-corporate messages. For instance, Apple's THINK DIFFERENT billboards showing the Dalai Lama have been transformed to read THINK DISILLUSIONED. More recently, culture jamming has hit the internet, especially through the practice of Google bombing: manipulating Google search results as a political statement. Typing the words "miserable failure" into the search engine, for example, calls up George W. Bush's official White House biography—as well as a BBC article on culture jamming.

CYBERSPACE (NOUN)

The virtual realm, accessed through the internet, populated by avatars and bots and viruses and worms.

The web is the most fully realized dimension of cyberspace, though the term predates the web by decades, originally used by sci-fi author William Gibson to describe "a consensual hallucination experienced daily by billions of legitimate operators, in every nation . . . like city lights, receding." The concept has grown to encompass every technological development from '70s virtual reality to present-day telepresence, and cyber- is used as a convenient prefix for online activities including cyberselling, cyberspying, and chat room cybersex. As our consensual hallucination broadens, the term *cyberspace* remains one of the few fixed beacons.

CYBORG (NOUN)

pronounced *SY-boorg*

A cybernetic organism.

Combining biology and robotics, merging natural and human-made components, cyborgs blur traditional distinctions between human and machine. Cyborgs have populated science fiction for at least the past century, figuring in *Star Trek* episodes and stories by Isaac Asimov, embodying human technolust as well as anxiety that our species is losing its identity to steel and silicon. In this sense, cyborgs are philosophical toys, fulfilling the role played by lifelike automata in the eighteenth century. More recently, cyborgs have, to a limited extent, become a reality: Prostheses such as artificial heart valves make people partly mechanical, and biobricks are the basic components for making living machines. The future of these hybrids, the degree of their societal acceptance, may owe as much to sci-fi as to advanced engineering.

DARKNET (NOUN)

A private filesharing network **that allows acquaintances to exchange music and other media surreptitiously over the internet.**

Such friend-to-friend (*F2F*) filesharing differs from everyday peer-to-peer (*P2P*) filesharing in the safeguards taken to prevent outsiders from accessing pirated materials or monitoring illegal activity: Because one user can access another user's computer only with prior permission, anybody not invited into the network by a member can never penetrate the darknet in the first place—and even those who are members can access the computers of users they don't know only through a secret chain of friends-in-common. Darknets have attracted hostility from media companies seeking to protect their intellectual property, and from law enforcement agencies wary of untraceable communication between terrorists. Less expectedly, darknets have been criticized by otherwise libertarian *netizens* (internet citizens) afraid that F2F, the digital equivalent of high school cliques, will irrevocably fragment the online world.

DATABASE (NOUN)

A digital **record-keeping system.**

If the assets of the information economy are data, then databases are the banks, not only providing safe storage but also adding value. With a database, useful relationships amongst data can be discovered. Marketers can mine databases for customers' buying patterns, for instance, and then track them by region to target advertising. Scientists can monitor correlations between drugs and side effects in clinical studies, and politicians can reverse engineer policy from popular opinion to take full advantage of polls. Like a solid banking firm, a well-designed database will support a whole range of transactions. Yet performance has as much to do with the database manager's skill at posing effective queries. For this reason, Oracle, the best-known database, is aptly named: The oracles of ancient Greece were informative only to those whose questions were well informed.

DATA MINING (NOUN)

Searching a large volume of data for meaningful patterns using an automated system such as a neural network.

The basic concept of data mining comes out of scholarship: A paleontologist might try to learn the fate of dinosaurs by sorting through the fossil record, and a historian might try to understand the social values of a bygone era by charting the marriage and divorce rates in old census documents. Since computers have become commonplace, the collection of data by governments, businesses, and even individuals has grown exponentially, requiring other machines to sort through the information, and to put it in terms that people can grasp. Data mining can help biochemists discover new drugs, but it's also used by law enforcement to monitor phone and internet records, invading privacy with unrivaled efficiency. Machines have no ethics, and people tend to discern patterns where they want to see them. As a result, *data dredging*—finding causality in coincidence—may be the most dangerous legal weapon of our age.

DATING (NOUN)

With the same dispassionate efficiency that online auction sites use to match prospective buyers and sellers, online dating services seek to pair prospective lovers.

Men and women post boastful profiles with flattering photos on sites such as Match.com, hoping to attract mates who will overlook the discrepancy between ad and reality. This generally happens because both parties exaggerate—bolstering salaries and belting waistlines—making due diligence the romantic equivalent of mutually assured destruction. The success of online dating services, which are among the web's most lucrative businesses, has less to do with computerized profile matching than with providing a space in which people can behave shamelessly under the guise of anonymity: While they may not be honest about who they are, they're usually straightforward about what they want, especially in so-called casual encounters listings, which might pass, in other circumstances, for pretty good pornography. Finding lasting love isn't equivalent to searching for home electronics on eBay, but for the planned obsolescence of most modern relationships, online dating services are ideal.

DEFAULT (NOUN OR ADJECTIVE)

Standard factory-programmed settings.

Computers and electronic devices come with a number of defaults, which reflect engineers' assumptions about end users' needs and tastes. In the case of software, there is generally a default language, usually English. On a TV, defaults may include color settings, generally garish. Most defaults can be adjusted with little effort, though only within a preset gamut. It's an engineer's world; we just live in it.

DESKTOP (NOUN)

While the desktop computer takes its name from the surface it rests on, the computer desktop takes its name from the environment it imitates.

Iconic folders store iconic documents until, with a drag of the proverbial mouse, they're dropped into an iconic trash bin. Designed to make computing intelligible to laymen a couple of decades ago (see next page), the imagery is more or less *sui generis* to a generation that has never handled the manila original.

THE DESKTOP METAPHOR

In 1984, on Super Bowl Sunday, Apple Computer ran a legendary onetime-only TV spot, showing a woman hurtling through a futuristic dystopia, pursued by uniformed authorities. At the last moment before her capture, she hurled a sledgehammer at the vast blue screen of an apparently omnipotent computer, escaping her Orwellian fate. "On January 24, Apple Computer will introduce Macintosh," an announcer intoned. "And you'll see why 1984 won't be like *1984*."

That the ad operated in such overtly metaphoric terms was apt, for it was with metaphor, rather than technology, that Apple made the computer accessible to anybody who cared to use one. How? By making it similar to the old-fashioned desktop. Gone was the need to memorize command lines, let alone programming languages as foreign to everyday life as Sanskrit. Managing data became as intuitive as manipulating physical files and folders. With the mouse as a prosthetic limb, anyone could get ahold of the computing power once hoarded by a technological elite.

Of course Apple didn't maintain monopoly control over the desktop revolution. Soon Microsoft had a Windows version, which narrowly avoided infringement on Apple's intellectual property rights by designing a desktop environment that looked less like a home office than a corporate cubicle. The metaphor has since become ubiquitous, sprawling across the web. An internet connection puts metaphoric libraries and multiplexes and grocery stores on the desktop. The situation would be ludicrous, except for the fact that it's strangely grounded in reality: The world now *is* to be found on the desktop, because the desktop, cleared of anachronistic files and folders, is merely a resting place for a globally networked computer.

Yet we must still ask whether living in a metaphor is any less Orwellian than embracing the dystopia of *1984*.

DESKTOP PUBLISHING (NOUN)

A generic term for the design and production of printed matter, from ads to newspapers, on a computer.

Desktop publishing originated as a marketing handle for Aldus PageMaker in 1985. Running on the minuscule black-and-white screen of the early Macintosh, PageMaker offered approximately the versatility and control of an Etch A Sketch. Current software, in contrast, is more flexible and precise than the finest hand typesetting (to which it is not easily compared, as desktop publishing has nearly driven typesetting to extinction). With an application such as Adobe InDesign, a designer can combine text and graphics to digitally create a billboard or a book without apprenticeship or assistance. The only limiting factor is imagination, which, given the generic look of most page layouts generated by people who mistake convenience for effectiveness, would be a highly marketable plug-in.

DIAL-UP (NOUN OR ADJECTIVE)

An internet hookup over a standard phone line, now largely replaced by broadband.

A dial-up connection between PC and service provider is made through a pair of modems, devices that convert digital signals to analog sounds and vice versa: In shrieks and squawks, the modems talk to each other over the same wire that carries telemarketing calls and spats between lovers. As in lovers' quarrels, there's a lag time in communication between machines that can cause anxiety, especially when split-second decisions in online auctions and gambling—easily negotiated over broadband—divide winners and losers.

DIGERATI [NOUN PLURAL]

The digital literati, a technological elite that invented the modern world, or at least engineered our perception of it.

Charter members, self-appointed or appointed by one another, include innovators (internet pioneer Vinton Cerf), tycoons (Apple CEO Steve Jobs), futurists (MIT Media Lab founder Nicholas Negroponte), popularizers (*New York Times* reporter John Markoff), and renegades (master hacker Kevin Mitnick). Nothing unites the digerati philosophically, yet collectively they have advanced the idea, scarcely challenged today, that the ills of society are essentially technical problems, to be solved with cheaper computer power and/or greater connectivity. Whatever may happen to the planet, one thing the digerati understand is how to protect their own future.

DIGITAL (ADJECTIVE)

A phenomenon or process expressed in numbers, often by a computer.

Most characteristics of the world, as experienced by humans, are continuous: As day fades into night, for instance, the temperature outside slides. Yet for purposes of communication or calculation, we make numeric approximations, counting in minutes or degrees. Computers likewise work digitally, recording, storing, and manipulating data in long strings of 1s and 0s known as *binary code*. The rigid simplicity of this format makes it ideal for computation, but problematic for human interaction: A digital picture or CD necessarily lacks the seamless gradation of reality.

DISTRIBUTED COMPUTING (NOUN)

High-power computing using machines connected over the internet.

Dedicated to the same task, many computers working in tandem may outperform individual supercomputers, especially when the task can be broken down into smaller independent problems. For example, the nearly five hundred thousand servers that collectively make up the Google search engine—rapidly processing an estimated two billion search requests daily—need not work together to perform any individual search. Distributed computing can even take advantage of downtime on privately owned PCs: The nearly one million computers volunteered for SETI@home, for instance, each sort through small batches of radiotelescope data during their free hours as part of a coordinated search for extraterrestrial intelligence. Running on code no more complicated than "think globally, act locally," they cumulatively have processing power equivalent to IBM's Blue Gene/L, the fastest computer in the world.

DOMAIN NAME (NOUN)

Uniquely identifying a website with a string of letters, a domain name is a company or institution's calling card in cyberspace.

Simple domain names such as Cars.com are coveted, and may even be traded for large sums of money, with Business.com selling for a record seven and a half million dollars at the height of the dotcom boom. For all that humans care about such matters, domain names are of no significance to computers, which are actually identified with numbers, known as *internet protocol addresses*, stored in directories to which computers must refer whether someone calls up www.whitehouse.gov or www.llanfairpwllgwyngyllgogerychwyrndrobwllllantysiliogogogoch.co.uk (the domain name for the Welsh village of Llanfairpwllgwyngyllgogerychwyrndrobwllllantysiliogogogoch, of course).

DOTCOM (NOUN)

Originally used to denote the .com suffix on business web addresses—distinguishing them from *.edu* schools and *.org* nonprofits—*dotcom* became the catchphrase for internet start-ups during the '90s boom.

Plummeting into bankruptcy following the dotcom crash in 2000, many of those start-ups came to be called "dotbombs." With billions of dollars in venture capital money lost on companies such as Pets.com (which inexplicably tried to sell dog and cat food on the internet), even dotcoms with intelligible business models such as eBay became wary of the *dotcom* moniker, and less likely to deride any company with physical assets as *bricks-and-mortar*. Only now, with the advent of domain names such as *.biz* and *.xxx*, is the bubble set to start filling again.

DVD (NOUN)

A digital versatile disc, popularly known as a "digital video disc" because most DVDs are used to distribute movies.

DVDs physically resemble CDs and operate on the same principle, yet they have storage capacity many times greater, providing far more space than most users need for archiving data. For film distribution, though, DVDs are ideal, cheap enough to be produced independently and compact enough to be sent through the mail by rental services such as Netflix—crucial factors in democratizing moviemaking.

E- (PREFIX)

The most common letter in the English language, *e* may also be the most prevalent prefix on the internet.

The letter *e* can be appended to anything electronic that has a nonelectronic antecedent. Email is the least of it. An e-student might study e-commerce in an e-book to learn about e-trading, or perhaps to work for a company such as eBay. In other words, just as electrons are subject to quantum fluctuation, *e* has no fixed meaning.

EASTER EGG [NOUN]

A hidden feature programmed into computer software, accessed using an obscure set of commands.

Often conceived as inside jokes by bored coders, Easter eggs may add a layer of unexpected play to even the most straightforward application: A flight simulator is embedded in early versions of Microsoft Excel, for instance, and cognoscenti can access a pinball game in Word 97 through the font menu. Easter eggs are also included in many computer games— and hunting for them or accidentally stumbling upon them is often more entertaining than the games themselves.

EMAIL (NOUN)

Electronic mail.

Over the two millennia since Augustus Caesar established a system for delivering messages by horseback in Rome, mail has been distributed by mule and pigeon, balloon and biplane. Yet none of these is as light or fast as the electron. As a result, with the establishment of the internet, email overwrote thousands of years of postal routes and practically put the venerable U.S. Postal Service into the business of selling commemorative stamps to teenagers. Yet the efficiency of email may be the cause of its demise: While junk mail from the likes of Publisher's Clearinghouse once arrived only intermittently, spam advertising under-the-table Viagra or fake Rolex watches is the primary content each morning in everybody's mailbox. Legislation to curb spam has proven practically useless—and the laws of physics governing the speed of subatomic particles have proven intractable.

EMOTICON (NOUN)

pronounced *ee-MOTE-a-con*

An emotive icon, such as a smile or a frown, inserted into email or chat room dialogue to substitute for the physical and aural cues of face-to-face communication.

Because English text runs from left to right, most emoticons are read in that way, often with a sidelong tilt of the head. The characters :-) may be used to suggest that the words preceding it should be read humorously, while annoyance is often expressed with the characters :-/, and :-* is used by some chat room romantics to send a kiss. Nearly every imaginable combination of characters means something within one or another online subculture, though the use of @=D to stand for Elvis or (_:^(l) to represent Homer Simpson can hardly be said to express nuances of meaning that might be missed in straight text. Whether a smiley face contributes more emotional depth than a well-turned phrase, on the other hand, remains open to interpretation.

EMULATOR (NOUN)

A program that lets a modern computer run antiquated software.

Old spreadsheets such as VisiCalc, and console games such as Asteroids, were written to run on primitive hardware. To make them compatible with the latest-generation PCs requires an extra layer to emulate the computer system for which they were originally written. Often the task is more challenging than writing code from scratch: Lacking documentation explaining exactly how old hardware worked, programmers have to reverse engineer the device. The mania for retrocomputing on the part of nostalgic Generation Xers, as much as the need of companies to access old ledgers, keeps emulation on the cutting edge of computing.

ENCRYPTION (NOUN)

Encoding sensitive information **sent over the internet, encryption makes the** web **safe for business.**

Techniques developed for wartime communication about enemy troop positions are now routinely used to conceal credit card numbers, and sophisticated ciphers historically classified by the government are fodder for discussion on internet forums. Those ciphers—essentially algorithms for scrambling bits of data—may be private key or public key. For *private* key ciphers to work, both sender and receiver must know how the code works by having shared a secret "key" in advance. *Public* key systems, such as Pretty Good Privacy (PGP), let everyone in on the secret of how to encode data, but keep the secret of how to decode it in house. In this way, passwords can be securely conveyed to e-commerce companies, and private enterprise can thrive in public.

ENHANCEMENT DIVIDE (NOUN)

The societal downside to artificial enhancement of physical or mental abilities by the affluent.

Advances in medicine to treat the ill or disabled, from pharmaceuticals to prosthetic limbs, have the potential to make healthy people superhuman. Just as the digital divide was supposed to doom those unable to access new technologies, the enhancement divide is predicted to render obsolete those without brain implants or infrared eyesight. As those technologies eventually become as affordable as a PC or cell phone, however, the greater threat to humanity may be the universal need to keep up with the bionic Joneses: Within a few generations, natural abilities may be a purely romantic notion wistfully evoked by a cyborg Rousseau.

ERGONOMICS (NOUN)

pronounced *erg-oh-NAH-mics*

Engineering for usability, ergonomics seeks to align the differing needs of human and machine.

While ergonomics originated as an attempt to shape human behavior for greater efficiency in factories, increasingly attention is paid to shaping technology to fit the natural contours of body and mind. Ergonomics has molded the computer mouse and keyboard to our hands, as well as the design of software to our intuition and attention span. (From the standpoint of a computer, desktop graphics are a waste of memory, yet they help us remember the tasks at hand.) As technology has become primarily the domain of consumer culture, ergonomics has succumbed to marketing, and often reflects our own uncertainty about what's best for us—whether we prefer a cell phone to be less weight in the pocket, for instance, or less strain on the eyes. *Hedonomics*, or design for pleasurability, addresses the challenge by setting aside usefulness in favor of designer colors.

FAQ (NOUN)

pronounced *fak*

Acronym for *frequently asked question*.

What is a FAQ? A FAQ is a list of questions and answers, posted on a website or newsgroup with boilerplate answers, to preemptively address newbie ignorance and confusion. How is *FAQ* pronounced? The correct pronunciation is *fak*, though some insist on spelling it out. Why are FAQs worth reading? A FAQ can save a newbie considerable time by providing information that could otherwise be learned only by lurking for days or weeks, and considerable embarrassment by heading off breaches of netiquette as obscure yet essential as *Robert's Rules of Order*. When are FAQs worth ignoring? A FAQ ought to be ignored when a commercial website uses it as an uncalled-for advertising campaign, drilling in propaganda about products with the tenacity of a catechism.

FEED (NOUN)

A news bulletin automatically delivered from web to computer.

Feed sources include news bureaus and blogs that offer syndication, a system for delivering updates to subscribers over the internet, much like mass email. Subscribers may collect and read those updates using a web browser or a more specialized application called an *aggregator*: Either way, the feeds subscribed to, and compiled by the day or minute, collectively amount to a personalized newspaper. One feed might provide local weather. Another might deliver specific stock quotes. And another might provide a daily horoscope. This can save an enormous amount of time, defining interests, eliminating distractions. Yet it can also narrow the knowledge of subscribers to approximately the width of a PDA.

FILESHARING (NOUN)

Communal distribution of digital media, especially music, over the internet.

Members of a filesharing network allow others to copy from their library in exchange for access to the libraries of others, effectively giving everyone every song that anyone purchases. Such generosity comes at the expense of musicians and recording companies, resulting in copyright infringement suits against centralized networks such as Napster (which was forced to pay $36 million in royalties following a 2001 ruling) and even individual traders (who have been tracked and penalized thousands of dollars for illegally trading files on Kazaa). Vigilance by the music industry has made Napster and Kazaa go legit, selling music instead of giving it away, and has driven much of their constituencies onto darknets where they can do what they've always done—infringe on copyrights, only with greater efficiency.

FILTER (NOUN)

Software for blocking internet access to websites deemed inappropriate by authorities ranging from parents to employers to governments.

Also known as *censorware*, internet filters, installed on computers or servers, discriminate based on keywords such as *sex* and *democracy*. As a result, they tend to be as bluntly literal as the reasoning of those who impose them on their children and workers and citizens. For instance, efforts to curtail access to pornography in public libraries by blocking sites containing the word *breast* have prevented patrons from researching breast cancer and learning new ways to barbecue chicken. In fact, the most successful use of censorware has been by totalitarian regimes, such as China, which aren't looking for an information filter so much as a cork.

FIREWALL [NOUN]

A system to protect a computer or network **from attack by** hackers**.**

Just as concrete barriers impede the spread of fire by compartmentalizing buildings, firewalls may help prevent a virus from completely overrunning the internet—yet firewalls are not typically built for collective safety. Maintained by IT specialists for corporations (and occasionally used by execs at home), they have more in common with medieval moats that protected the inhabitants of castles even as war and disease decimated the countryside. Networks protected by firewalls are less vulnerable than the internet as a whole. However, without a healthy internet, equally open to everyone, insulated businesses may find themselves as isolated as palaces without villages.

FLAME WAR (NOUN)

An argument for the sake of argument, sudden and violent, between people whose emotional lives are lived online.

Flame wars are common occurrences on internet forums ostensibly set up for serious discussion of substantive issues. Online communities tend to blame trolls for flame wars, while psychologists generally maintain that flame wars are caused by miscommunication. (One study claims that people are able to discern whether a written comment is meant ironically merely 50 percent of the time.) However, the frequency and vehemence of flame wars suggests that, like wrestling between children, they have more to do with recreation.

FOLKSONOMY (NOUN)

pronounced *folk-SAHN-a-mee*

A folk taxonomy, the cumulative effort of an online community to classify web content inaccessible to Google.

Designed to find words in documents, search engines cannot detect objects in photographs, for instance, or actions in films. *Folksonomy* is a term for a set of tags people apply to that imagery on social bookmarking sites such as del.icio.us (where millions of pictures can be searched and sorted by their folksonomy of tags). There are no rules: One person might tag a snapshot of a sleeping tabby with the word *cat*, another might write *nap*, and another might note the *quilt* on which it's *cutely snoozing*. Over time, though, the bookmarks amount to a representation of how the photo is collectively perceived, not at all the systematic description that would be given by a librarian but one that serves the unsystematic community. Folksonomies are sloppy and redundant, yet inherently useful because they're natural by-products of their users.

FONT (NOUN)

A digital typeface.

The word *font* refers to the pouring of molten lead to create movable type, an obsolete process foreign to modern graphic designers, who seldom even encounter a printing press. In fact, most typographic terms used in desktop publishing are quaintly antiquated, including *leading*, which once referred to the placement of lead between lines of type for spacing, and *upper-* and *lowercase*, which originally described the positioning of type trays. Despite this terminology, and despite the centuries-old pedigree of popular typefaces such as Caslon and Garamond, digital fonts have flexibility undreamed of by Gutenberg. They can be stretched and scaled to any size, and wholly new designs can be created on a computer with minimal hassle. Most of these are novelty fonts, made to look like handwriting or old-fashioned printing, and almost immediately go out of fashion—another concept that old Gutenberg wouldn't have understood.

FORUM (NOUN)

An online discussion group.

Devoted to a specific subject, such as lowriding or teddy bear collecting, a forum is a website comprising written exchanges among members, sometimes managed by a moderator. Exchanges are arranged by subtopics called threads. For instance, a lowriding forum might have a thread devoted to Series-31 Trojan batteries. On each thread, posts by members are archived chronologically, preserving for posterity valuable historical information about the 1909 Steiff center-seam teddy bear, for example, or a vicious argument over the best way to modify the speaking voice of Teddy Ruxpin to sound like Papa Smurf. The forum serves a social function similar to the chat room, without the need for quick typing. Ideally, this leads to more considered discussion, but often it merely facilitates more elaborate flame wars.

FRAZZING (NOUN)

Frenzied multitasking, as occurs when the combined output of cell phone, PDA, and laptop overwhelms the processing power of the human brain.

The term *multitasking* is computer jargon in its own right: By rapidly switching back and forth between jobs according to a precisely scheduled rotation, a PC can appear to do several jobs at once. Humans multitask when they emulate their machines, though few can do it all day long, especially as the number of electronic devices grows, and people feel compelled to read personal email on their laptops while reviewing travel scheduling on their PDA and pitching new business on their cells. Short-circuiting concentration, frazzing is the temporary insanity of the ADD generation.

FRONT END (NOUN)

**Everything visible on the computer screen, as opposed to the
underlying code that users never see.**

Just as many businesses have a front office decorated to impress clients
and a stripped-down back office where real work gets done, computer
systems have a front end that makes back-end processing presentable.
Programmers often disparage the front end, deeming it deceptive and
considering those who use it deficient. Without a front end, however, the
back end would be powerless: Few people would ever even plug in the
computer.

GAMBLING (NOUN)

A multibillion-dollar online industry, equaled in popularity only by porn.

Internet casinos offer all the standard games—craps and poker and roulette and baccarat—without the hassle of catching a Greyhound to Las Vegas, let alone the expense of jetting to Monte Carlo. Registered in Caribbean countries such as Antigua, the casinos are outside the reach of U.S. gaming codes, and the legality of gambling online is highly contentious, fraught with contradictory court rulings reflecting the confusion inevitable when territorial laws are applied to borderless cyberspace. Most gamblers are less worried about governmental threats than about the risks of dealing with casinos that digitally manipulate the odds, or with bots that play cards with the cool efficiency of computers.

GEEK (NOUN)

Technically adept and socially inept, the geek is the archetype of the digital age.

Derogatory use of the term—which originally referred to a species of circus freak—has diminished as geeks such as Bill Gates have become titans of the new economy, and as long-tail technologies such as the internet have nurtured the eccentric interests of the masses, previously exposed primarily to mainstream culture. Like nerds and wonks, geeks are single minded in their obsessions (which may run the gamut from operating system design to celluloid film preservation). However, while nerds advance their fields, and wonks manage day-to-day affairs, geeks may simply be fellow travelers. For this reason, geekiness is more a social phenomenon than an intellectual trait, an elitism that is open to everyone.

GEOCODING (NOUN)

The geographic encoding of web content.

Geocoding lets people google restaurants by region, for instance, or lets them locate every Laundromat in a neighborhood, and allows a search engine to show results on a map. Worldwide in scope, the web was built to make resources in Osaka or Oslo as readily accessible as those in Omaha, but until Google develops a teleportation device, human users have no choice but to be provincial.

GOD GAME (NOUN)

A computer game **in which the player manages the lives of onscreen characters or controls the conditions of an online world.**

The aerial view of most god games is consistent with the player's omnipotent position, and the player's degree of remove from the world as experienced by inhabitants. As any reader of Genesis knows, through omnipotence is no guarantee of success for a divinity: While there's no way to win or lose a game such as SimEarth (a simulation of the entire world, in which whole civilizations can be manipulated), controlling environmental factors to maintain a livable planet is considerably more difficult than killing a bunch of aliens in a shoot-em-up. Even smaller domains of influence can tax an aspiring deity: In The Sims, dubbed a "digital dollhouse" by creator Will Wright, the family for whom the player is responsible will have their house repossessed if the player doesn't regularly instruct them to pay their bills.

GOOGLE (NOUN OR VERB)

pronounced *GOO-gul*

The name of the world's most popular search engine.

Google has become a generic term for searching the web: Googling "Noah Webster" simply means searching the web for pages containing the lexicographer's name. This may be done using Yahoo! or AltaVista, but with an estimated market share of 80 percent, Google will more likely than not be the search engine selected. Originating as an accidental misspelling of *googol*, the mathematical term for the number 1×10^{100}, *google* is now practically a googol times more commonplace in conversation, and has even been included as a verb in *Webster's Dictionary.*

GOOGLAGE

The difference between the old and new economy can be represented in two words: *xerox* and *google*. Both are the trademarked names of global corporations, and both are used as generic verbs, yet Xerox considers *xeroxing* an actionable infringement, while Google deems *googling* an unpaid advertisement.

The distinction comes down to medium, the difference between atoms and bits. When Xerox came of age, early in the twentieth century, marketing was done in print, where it was expensive and scarce. By the time Google came of age, early in the twenty-first, marketing was moving onto the internet, where it's cheap and ubiquitous. Xerox could count on significant response if the company bought an ad in *The New York Times*. Google, on the other hand, could plaster ads all over the web at almost no cost and expect to be more or less ignored. In our media-saturated world, marketing depends on public participation. Xerox informed us about Xerox. We inform one another about Google.

And that requires a new conception of branding, often given the buzzword *viral marketing*, at which Google is an acknowledged master. A whole lexicon of google words can now be found (by googling them, naturally). *Googlage* is the acreage of cyberspace occupied by a given search term: For instance, Google has approximately one and a half times the googlage of Xerox. If two people have the same name, they're *googlegangers*: Google "Bill Wyman" and you find both the rock musician and the newspaper journalist whom the former sued—creature of the old economy—for sharing his superstar moniker.

Many companies, if not most, now depend on viral marketing of one kind or another. Often it's a matter of creating online content ludicrous enough to make people blog about it. Burger King's "Subservient Chicken" campaign is a classic example of this: Over a period of many months, somebody in a chicken suit followed orders from anyone who sent them in via a live web feed. (The idea ostensibly was to illustrate Burger King's "Have It Your Way" slogan.) Google has taken a similarly irreverent tone with annual April Fools' jokes, including the alleged expansion of the company to the moon.

Yet even earthbound expansion can affect a company. Google has recently started trying to recall its trademark from open use by sending warning letters to publications including *The Washington Post*. Google argues in these letters that such slippage amounts to "genericide," the fate of the escalator (originally a trademark of the Otis Elevator Company) and the mimeograph (once a trademark held by Thomas Edison). Perhaps it's a sign that the new economy is aging: Pioneering Google is the first company to inoculate itself against its own viral marketing.

GPS (NOUN)

An acronym for "Global Positioning System."

GPS is a constellation of twenty-four satellites that collectively provide navigational information to missiles and airplanes and well-heeled hikers and drivers who like having directions read to them by a voice simulator. The satellites all continuously broadcast their position in orbit, allowing a GPS receiver to measure latitude, longitude, and altitude more accurately than the finest sextant. The system was developed by the U.S. military for precision bombing, and civilian use was initially undermined by intentional distortion: The military programmed its satellites to deliver signals hundreds of yards from true. People with receivers in their cars or pockets need no longer worry about running into walls, though, unless they happen to be wandering through Baghdad: The Pentagon has developed ways to jam GPS signals selectively.

GUI (NOUN)

A graphical user interface, such as the desktop environment of Macintosh and Windows operating systems.

GUIs serve as translators between human and computer—allowing people to access files or browse the web intuitively—simulating familiar attributes of the physical world on screen. Graphical elements, such as buttons and scroll bars, are physically manipulated with a mouse, obviating the need to know anything about how the computer actually works. The web and the PC owe their popularity to the GUI, yet the GUI is also responsible for the widening divide between programmer and end user, rendering computers more mysterious even as they become more commonplace.

HACKER (NOUN)

A person who is mystifyingly proficient with technology.

A hacker may be a master programmer, such as world wide web inventor Tim Berners-Lee, or a criminal capable of infiltrating high-security computer systems, such as convicted felon Kevin Mitnick, who was found guilty of hacking into the computer system of Motorola and other companies. While the coding community tends to prefer the former definition, the public thinks of hackers in terms of the latter. This has been the case at least since the movie *WarGames* broadcast the word in the first place, and attempts by the digerati to popularize the term *cracker* for criminal *hackers* have failed utterly. The ambiguity of *hacker* may be appropriate, though: While a student at Oxford, Berners-Lee was banned from using the computer system after being caught trying to hack in, and Mitnick is now a respected computer security expert. Moreover, many in the open source community would say that illegally hacking proprietary software is a public service.

HARDWARE [NOUN]

The physical bulk of a computer.

External components such as keyboard and monitor may be referred to as hardware, but the term is most often used to distinguish between the computer's hardwired circuitry and the interchangeable programs that run on it, collectively called software. A PC's hardware comprises integrated circuits arranged on a motherboard, which can support a nearly unlimited range of software, just as the neural networks of the brain can support the mind's practically limitless thinking. However, just as the distinction between mind and brain is indefinite—and neither is truly independent—hardware and software are distinct only in theory: Software bears the mark of the hardware for which it was designed, and if that circuitry is no longer available, the hardware will have to be emulated for the software to operate properly.

HDTV (NOUN)

High-definition television.

While the realism of television programming has not appreciably increased over the past half century, resolution has more than doubled in the last few years alone thanks to improvements in broadcast and screen technology: Digital signals carry a vast amount of visual information, delivered onto monitors packed with pixels. Is it any wonder that so many people spend so much time indoors when the pictures on their TVs are so much clearer than their smog-filled cities?

HIT (NOUN)

The simplest measurement of a website's public standing, the number of hits corresponds to the number of files viewed by visitors.

Because many web pages are built from a large number of files, companies paying for banner ad placement are more likely to care about the total number of page views, or the total number of unique visitors, both of which can be tracked with debatable accuracy. Still, hits remain the currency of popularity in the world at large, where people raised on blockbusters and platinum records are more impressed by big numbers than by what they mean.

HOMEPAGE (NOUN)

Like the cover of a book, the homepage of a website is meant to evoke, elegantly and succinctly, the site's content through a combination of imagery and text.

And like most covers of most books, most homepages would make a graphic designer blanch. Institutional homepages generally follow the structure and style of a textbook's index, cataloging every iota of content in the same bland font. Corporate homepages tend to follow the model of direct-mail advertising, overwhelming visitors with cliché-ridden bombast. And personal homepages, on social networking sites such as MySpace, usually mirror yearbook pages, including photos with friends and lists of favorite bands. Which is to say that, while neither elegant nor succinct, most homepages do evoke their websites' content.

HYPERTEXT (NOUN)

Words or images connected to other, associated material elsewhere on the internet, instantly called up at the click of a mouse.

Like billions of overlapping strings, hypertext weaves the world wide web by linking sites with related content across institutions and continents. The concept of hypertext predates the technology by many centuries, in the footnoted references that kept scholars busy calling up tome after tome in the library. Hypertext automates the process and broadens it, allowing anyone anywhere to navigate the web's billions of pages, and to interlink new content using *HTML* (hypertext markup language). Hypertext counterbalances searchability, which narrows down the scope of the web to a specific subject: Hyperlinks provide a multiplicity of paths extending from an area of interest, tempting broader, more serendipitous exploration.

ICON (NOUN)

A pictogram on a computer desktop **symbolizing a** software application **or function.**

Whereas religious icons serve to enhance mystical experience, computer icons are designed to demystify PC operation. This is accomplished primarily by representing objects and ideas as literally as possible: Photo editing software might be signified by a camera icon, for example, and a search function might be characterized by an image of a magnifying glass. Of course, as any religion scholar knows, the iconic changes as tastes and styles evolve. On the Macintosh, for instance, unwanted files were once dragged into an industrial-strength aluminum trash can. Now the documents are deposited in a chic wire-mesh wastebasket.

IDENTITY THEFT (NOUN)

Impersonation for purposes of fraud.

Opportunities for identity theft have expanded with the internet, transforming the activity into a $50 billion industry with annual growth the envy of any legitimate e-business. Phishing and pharming have proven far more efficient than old-fashioned Dumpster diving for nabbing credit card and Social Security information, and online transactions, fast and anonymous, are far more efficient than passing phony checks at the corner market. If avatars represent the imaginative potential of the internet, identity theft demonstrates the risks of online disembodiment.

IM (NOUN OR VERB)

Instant messaging.

Combining qualities of email and phone conversation, IM allows people to converse using their keyboards instead of their vocal cords. IM is like chat room discussion, only private. Discussion is live, in the sense that text is sent over the internet as it's typed, yet, like email, exchanges are archived, making them searchable for future reference. As a result, IM is popular with both teenagers and businesses: For teens using AOL Instant Messenger, the technology offers the instant gratification of passing notes in class, while companies find Lotus Sametime ever-so-much easier than phone records for keeping tabs on transactions and employees. Moreover, both audiences can appreciate the potential for multitasking. Skilled teens can IM with three or four friends while watching TV, playing a shoot-em-up, and eating. Many employees, especially those who telecommute, have learned to do the same.

INFORMATION (NOUN OR ADJECTIVE)

Facts organized for a purpose.

Information is the primary commodity of our age, mined from raw data and traded as intellectual property. Unlike iron ore, though, more data doesn't necessarily yield more information. On the contrary, the exponential growth in data, as memory has become cheaper, has made information harder to find and more scarce. Moreover, because information is specific to a question, it's less lasting than the least stable isotope, dissolving into data again the moment that the question has been addressed or forgotten.

INKJET (NOUN OR ADJECTIVE)

A common liquid-based computer printer technology.

Minuscule droplets of colored ink are sprayed through moving nozzles onto a sheet of paper as it passes through the printer. With coated papers, inkjet images can be nearly as sharp as color photographs, yet they have a tendency to fade with extended exposure to light, like last year's killer app. Some industrial inkjets avoid this shortcoming by using special pigments, similar to acrylic paints, which can be sprayed onto large sheets of vinyl or canvas as well as paper, an advance embraced by artists seeking to make paintings in quantity without ever getting their brushes dirty. Biologists have also recently become interested in the high-precision potential of inkjet technology, printing living tissues, layer by layer, with cell cultures suspended in liquid. Organs are next, though copyright issues have yet to be worked out.

INTEGRATED CIRCUIT (IC) (NOUN)

A computer chip.

Replacing rooms full of vacuum tubes interconnected with miles of cable, ICs made modern technology possible, and continue to facilitate advances in computing at the staggering rate predicted more than four decades ago by Moore's Law. Unlike old-fashioned electronic circuits that had to be soldered together, ICs are etched into silicon wafers using an automated process that makes them cheap and reliable—qualities essential to the broad distribution of PCs and the development of the internet. Equally important, the microscopic scale of components improves their efficiency, making more powerful machines and mobile devices that can run on batteries. Nevertheless, the miniaturization of ICs is limited by the size of atoms, which even engineers cannot scale down. Not to be deterred, the most intrepid are beginning to research *quantum computing*, which enlists the strange qualities of subatomic particles.

INTERACTIVITY (NOUN)

Human–machine engagement.

Interactive content places spectators in a working role: Unlike television, the outcome of a computer game is the direct result of players' behavior in the game environment. A marketing buzzword, interactivity is now standard in both entertainment and education, appeasing attention-deficient audiences by allowing them to reshuffle preordained events. Enthusiasts prefer getting lost in even the most superficial immersive environments to being ushered through the complexities of a well-told story.

IT (NOUN OR ADJECTIVE)

An acronym for "information technology."

IT is a professional field concerned with configuring and maintaining computer systems. However, most people use *IT* as shorthand for "IT specialist," the person responsible for keeping systems running in organizations otherwise less computer-literate than the average kindergarten class. In this instance, the term may rightly be considered an expletive, for such systems are seldom mentioned unless they break down and require emergency intervention.

JOYSTICK (NOUN)

A video game control, deriving both name and design from the
joysticks used to fly airplanes in the World War I era, and later.

Almost ubiquitous in '80s video arcades, and standard with early consoles
such as the Atari, the joystick has remained popular even as gameplay has
migrated largely to the PC. More easily gripped than a mouse in the excite-
ment of virtual assault, the joystick maintains a battle-hardened profile that
the home- and office-bound mouse never had.

KIOSK (NOUN)

pronounced *KEE-osk*

A computer-cum-self-serve-information-booth.

The kiosk is the know-it-all cousin of the ATM, freely offering facts and figures 24/7. Not that digital kiosks are set up to reveal the meaning of life: Most are restricted to dispensing directions in public squares or delivering sales pitches at trade shows, in response to simple queries entered on colorful flashing touchscreens (heat-sensitive monitors that double as keyboards). Even though computerized kiosks are generally wired to the internet like an ordinary PC, the linked touch-screen options ensure that the economic interests of the operator—whether municipal or commercial—override the curiosity of the user.

LANGUAGE (NOUN)

A computer coding dialect.

To make a computer function, a programmer must write commands in a language that the machine can comprehend. Thousands of languages, from Lisp to Java to C++, have been developed over the past half century, each with a distinct grammar and vocabulary. Just as a plumber's tools and techniques are fit for working with pipes but would hinder a cobbler using them to make shoes, a language efficient for artificial intelligence might be problematic for search engines. Assembly languages, which work at the level of the circuitry, are the most flexible yet labor-intensive, the equivalent of working with the most basic wrench. Higher-level models such as scripting languages, which control the behavior of a computer with a few succinct commands, are both more and less powerful, like a contractor beholden to the plumber he orders to install a sink.

LAPTOP (NOUN)

A computer small enough to fit on a lap.

Optimized to run for three or more hours on rechargeable batteries, laptops are also called *notebooks*, reflecting their trim dimensions and also suggesting their casual use on planes and buses and in classrooms. They may soon even become as disposable as notebooks: Prototypes of a hundred-dollar laptop, developed for children in third-world countries, demonstrate that the hardware hardly matters anymore. What counts is internet access.

LASER PRINTER (NOUN)

A high-speed computer printer that uses a laser beam to transfer text and imagery from PC desktop to plain paper.

The first laser printer, built in 1971, was a modified Xerox machine, and all laser printers since have applied the basic concepts of xerography: A beam of light scans an image onto an electrostatically charged drum, reversing the charge wherever the light hits. In places where the electrostatic charge remains unchanged, the drum picks up finely powdered ink (called *toner*) and rolls it onto a sheet of paper. The toner is then melted under a heat lamp, binding permanently to the page. Like Xerox machines, laser printers can now produce images in full color, and like Xeroxes they run cleanly until someone opens the lid to change the toner . . . and comes out looking like an industrial-age factory worker.

LEETSPEAK [NOUN]

Text intentionally distorted and/or abbreviated to be readable only to an online elite.

The word *leet* (or l33t) itself is an example of leetspeak, a version of the English word *elite*, shortened to one syllable and rendered phonetically, sometimes with numbers or other symbols substituted for the letters that they loosely resemble. At the extreme, leetspeak is utterly illegible to the uninitiated. For instance, nobody trained on an IBM Selectric would ever guess that "+I-I3 q(_)1(I< I3r0\/\/I\I ph0x j(_)/\/\p5 0\/3r +I-I3 I_@z`/ I)06" stands for "the quick brown fox jumps over the lazy dog." Originating as a typographic shorthand, leetspeak evolved into a means of signifying membership in the hacker (or *haxor*) community, a linguistic barrier to newbies (or *n00bs*). Still sometimes used by teens to keep parents from reading their text messages, leetspeak is now primarily employed by spammers selling W1ndOws 2OOO or Natura1 Pen1s en1argement pi11z, product offers readable to any sentient being—just not to a computer spam filter.

LEGACY SYSTEM (NOUN)

Aging technology that has become so integral to day-to-day operations that it cannot practically be replaced.

Organizations that require constant access to data, such as banks and insurance companies, often maintain computer hardware and software built by companies that have gone out of business, or designed by employees who have left the industry. Firmly entrenched and poorly understood, systems that initially empowered organizations ultimately control them. In this sense they are similar to the human body, which in youth is a release and in old age is a coffin.

LIFEHACK (NOUN OR VERB)

Any technique that makes life easier is termed a lifehack by people who live their lives on the computer.

The word was first used to describe programming tricks that coders shared with one another, yet has since grown to include ideas about how to have an argument (be direct) and how to alleviate back pain (take a walk around the block). Obvious to anybody who gets out, these tips are traded on websites such as Lifehacker.com, alongside advice about what to feed your cat in an emergency (Cheerios and june bugs), which collectively suggest that the best idea would be to unplug the PC forever.

LINK (NOUN OR VERB)

The structural underpinnings of the world wide web, links interconnect web pages based on related content.

Any website can be directly referenced by any other in hypertext markup language (HTML): A click of the mouse will instantly call up the referenced URL. If a website is not actively maintained, the link may reference a URL that has gone out of date, a problem known as link rot. Nevertheless, most links are preserved indefinitely because links are the basis of popularity on the web, and are the primary standard by which search engines rate which websites are important.

LISTSERV (NOUN)

An email discussion group, devoted to a given subject, such as library science or *The Sopranos*.

Subscribers to a listserv converse by posting information or gossip to the entire group via an automated email distribution hub called a *reflector*. Anyone can reply to any message, meaning that a passing comment can generate boxes of response. For this reason, subscribers may choose to receive daily digests, containing all exchanges in a single easy-to-delete email. However, receiving each message piecemeal is an efficient way to simulate an active social life.

LONG TAIL (NOUN)

The aggregate popularity of individually-unpopular phenomena.

Blockbusters may claim the majority of mainstream media attention, but obscure art films and documentaries, quietly distributed over the internet, collectively have a larger audience. Taken from statistics and popularized in *Wired* magazine by editor in chief Chris Anderson, the long tail accounts for this tendency, and explains the success of companies such as Netflix, which stock millions of titles, orders of magnitude more than can possibly be contained in the largest video store. Long-tail distributions are found in every realm of e-commerce, and on the web more broadly: Most blogs are unpopular, read by very few people, yet most people read unpopular blogs. Offering nearly endless variety, distributed almost effortlessly, the internet monetizes eccentricity.

LUDDITE (NOUN OR ADJECTIVE)

pronounced *LUDD-ite*

An opponent of technology for technology's sake.

Anachronistic by temperament—tending to prefer pen and paper to word processor, library to internet café, concert hall to MP3 file—Luddites even take their name from the past. The original Luddites were early-nineteenth-century mill workers who sabotaged newly introduced wide-frame looms that they believed threatened their livelihoods. Self-professed followers of Ned Ludd, a mythical eighteenth-century laborer, they stood in the way of the industrial revolution with predictable results: Endorsement by Lord Byron, followed by death or deportation. More than their weaving skills, their martyrdom appeals to Luddites today, whose romantic embrace of a lost cause is the ultimate stance against our progress-driven, relentlessly technological society.

LUDOLOGY (NOUN)

pronounced *lood-OLL-o-jee*

The academic study of video games.

Taking its name from the Latin word for "game," and deriving techniques from literary and film theory, ludology seeks to analyze the narrative structures of popular games, from Grand Theft Auto (in which players act as urban criminals) to EverQuest (in which players act as Old World sorcerers), as well as to characterize how players experience them. While unlikely to affect game sales, such scholarship does bolster college humanities enrollment, much as game-design classes have been a boon for visual arts departments.

LURKER (NOUN)

pronounced *LURK-er*

A person who watches online community activity, but does not participate in it.

Like Jane Goodall observing chimpanzees in the field, the lurker learns the customs of an online community by watching activity without joining in. Unlike Jane Goodall, the lurker generally does so in order to join the community without behaving foolishly. (Those who contribute to a discussion forum without lurking first will often be flamed for stating the obvious, that being the privilege of seasoned participants.) For all the talk of democracy, internet communities are more stratified than a medieval village, or the faculty of any Ivy League college.

MACHINIMA (NOUN)

pronounced *ma-SHEEN-i-mah*

A combination of the words *machine* and *cinema*, machinima is a technique for making cheap animated films using 3-D computer games.

Stories are told by guiding the actions of game characters, recorded on a PC and uploaded for viewing on websites with massive underground audiences such as Machinima.com. Scenarios usually have nothing to do with gameplay. Like resourceful indie directors who film on the street rather than building sets, machinima artists appropriate preexisting virtual worlds for their own filmic purposes.

MACRO (NOUN)

An automated shortcut for a routine task.

The first macros were developed by scriptwriters to format screenplays produced on a word processor: A standard set of procedures, such as spacing and indentation, could be reduced to a single keystroke. Macros are still used to play out strings of commands in a wide range of applications and even computer games. And the monotony of Hollywood makes one wonder whether a supermacro has been developed to write and produce entire movies.

MAINFRAME (NOUN OR ADJECTIVE)

An industrial-strength computer.

Predating the PC by decades, the mainframe has endured for essentially the same reasons that farm tractors haven't been put out of work by weed whackers: Mainframes can reliably perform repetitive tasks such as credit card processing for years on end, jobs that justify costly computers because the expense of downtime is prohibitive. Mainframes may also be used as corporate web servers, but their rigidity does not take well to creative work such as weather forecasting and cryptography, tasks better performed by prodigy supercomputers.

MANULARITY (NOUN)

pronounced *man-yoo-LAIR-i-tee*

The opposite of automation.

The term is used sarcastically by hackers to describe the labor involved in any task undertaken by hand that might more efficiently have been completed by machine. Balancing a checkbook on paper or handwriting a letter involves a degree of manularity that is incomprehensible to a generation raised on spreadsheets and word processors. Nevertheless, in their effort to decrease the manularity of straightforward tasks, true techies will often, as a point of honor, devise solutions of a time-consuming complexity that would make Rube Goldberg reach for his fountain pen.

MASH-UP [NOUN]

A combination of the vocals from one song with the instrumentals from another.

Mash-ups are remixes for the MP3 era, in which all music is available through filesharing and every teenager is a DJ. Madonna has been crossed with the Sex Pistols and Eminem's voice has been layered over AC/DC and Vanilla Ice. While the music industry has fought the trend with cease-and-desist boilerplate—ignoring creative antecedents in hip-hop and even classical music—the term *mash-up* has bolstered the phenomenon, and now encompasses video and software remixes. The real estate listings on Craigslist, for instance, can be plotted onto Google maps. Such applications are undoubtedly useful, even if the only conceivable reason to call them mash-ups is to lend them hipster appeal.

MEDIA ART (NOUN)

Art created using new technologies, including computers and the internet.

Originating in the '60s as a challenge to the hegemony of oil on canvas, media art has tantalized museum audiences with immersive experiences and tormented them with futuristic anxieties. While much media art merely takes advantage of the latest engineering, amounting to little more than a demo of a novel virtual reality environment or 3-D rendering technique, the great talents, from Nam June Paik to Ken Goldberg, seamlessly integrate technological source and subject. Paik's 1974 *TV Garden*, for instance, set televisions in a thicket of tropical plants, suggesting the new flowering of an artificial hybrid. More recently, Goldberg's *Telegarden* allowed volunteers to tend a small plot of land over the internet by maneuvering a robotic arm, reaching toward the limits of virtual community.

MEME (NOUN)

pronounced *meem*

A self-perpetuating idea.

Replicating and mutating through human communication, memes are similar to genes, and subject to equivalent evolutionary processes. For instance, a religion may be carried by a population of believers, each of whom may have slightly different notions about ritual and liturgy. Over many generations, small differences may amount to major divisions (as in Christianity), or distinct belief systems may merge (as in Taoist Buddhism). The internet has accelerated the propagation of memes, vastly increasing their number and diminishing the impact of each. Internet memes are often fads (e.g., the dotcom boom) or rumors (e.g., the urban legend about meticulously pruned bonsai kittens). Among the most prevalent memes on the internet is the notion of a meme in its own right, a concept introduced by biologist Richard Dawkins in 1976 that didn't enter popular culture until the '90s, when the web provided an ecosystem in which memetics could flourish.

MEMETICS

Google "brrreeeport" and you get more than 130,000 hits, an enviable number, especially given that brrreeeport isn't the name of anybody famous or a popular place. It isn't even a common typo. The fact is that brrreeeport doesn't exist, except as a meme on the internet.

Brrreeeport came into existence—if *existence* is the right word for it—on February 14, 2006, when a blogger named Robert Scoble wrote the following: "Here, let's play a game. Everyone in the world say 'brrreeeport' on your blog." Within minutes, his readers were doing so, and their readers, too. Soon brrreeeport was generating more interest than Dick Cheney's infamous February 13 hunting mishap. By February 16, *The Village Voice* had gratuitously worked the word into the headline for a music review. Within a few more days, people had registered the domain names brrreeeport.com and brrreeeport.co.uk, hoping to capitalize on the publicity that the term was unexpectedly generating.

Scoble was not the first to introduce a word as a means of examining the workings of the internet. German web designers were using *schnitzelmitkartoffelsalat*—literally "schnitzel with potato salad"—as a term to test how their sites fared on search engines as early as 2002, and have since held contests to see who can get the highest search engine ranking. *Brrreeeport* was proposed partly in the same spirit, and also as a means for unknown blogs to get notice: With the influx of people looking up "brrreeeport," any blog that mentioned it was likely to get a bit of attention.

Yet *brrreeeport* reached well beyond the blogosphere to become a shibboleth for anyone attuned to pop culture. That's why *The Village Voice* used it, and why people continue to throw it in, meaninglessly, on a blog or web page. It's a true meme, arguably the purest meme, since it was created simply to be repeated. Thus Scoble's stunt became a social experiment.

And the results? *Brrreeeport* reached its peak on search engines approximately six months after the word was invented, and has been gradually fading ever since. It dwindled as it became commonplace. Even memes, it seems, are subject to laws of supply and demand.

MEMORY (NOUN)

The data store of a computer.

Like humans, computers function on both short-term and long-term memory. Short-term memory, usually RAM, provides a computer with the set of instructions needed to undertake a given routine, such as how to play an MP3 file as music. Long-term memory contains all the information—from MP3 files to reference libraries—processed by software in short-term memory, as well as permanent copies of the software itself. This data may be stored magnetically on the computer, or optically on CDs. The largest memory bank in the world, though, is the internet, which by one estimate contains the amount of information that could be written on the paper made from five million trees. A single CD, even, could store the complete works of a hundred Shakespeares. The cost of that CD might be a couple of cents, and storage on the internet is often offered for free. With memory so cheap and abundant, the challenge increasingly is to find something worth remembering.

MEMS (NOUN)

An acronym for "microelectromechanical systems."

MEMS refers to a growing class of microscopic motors and levers, devices with moving parts fabricated using technologies adapted from computer chip manufacture. MEMS inside car tires monitor air pressure, and MEMS inside inkjet printers spray paper with minuscule droplets of pigment, producing intricate pictures. MEMS are most coveted for their potential to manufacture new molecules, such as drugs, a feat that will first require microelectromechanical factories to build smaller MEMS called NEMS: nanoelectromechanical systems.

MENU (NOUN OR ADJECTIVE)

A list of command options for a software application.

Menu bars are onscreen control panels, manipulated with a mouse. Because all possible actions are explicitly stated, menus let users work with software before learning how it works. However, working by trial and error from options found on menu bars is a far cry from mastering the software, just as ordering off a menu at a restaurant isn't the same as knowing how to cook.

METADATA [NOUN]

Data about data.

Like the tab on a manila folder, metadata provides a uniform summary of a digital file, regardless of category or format, telling people what the file contains and showing machines how to read it. Metadata such as information about when a file was created, or who wrote it, make data more readily searchable—a crucial function given the amount of data generated every day. Naturally, the amount of metadata generated to support that data has increased the demand for meta-metadata: The more paperless the office, the longer the paper trail.

MICROCHUNK (VERB)

To split up a product or service traditionally sold as a package, offering each piece to buyers *à la carte*.

For instance, someone might purchase individual songs through iTunes rather than a whole album from Amazon. Applying the Ikea philosophy to everything from home electronics to news feeds, microchunking allows consumers to customize their total living environment, seeing only what they want to see and hearing only what they want to hear, on audio/video systems comprising components that all have the same look and color as their home decor. While some commentators have cautioned that this might isolate individuals, depriving contemporary society of a cultural commons, the fact that most Ikea-furnished homes look more or less the same suggests that microchunking may just be a clever method of mass marketing in a time when everyone wants to appear unique.

MMORPG (NOUN)

An acronym for a "massively multiplayer online role-playing game."

MMORPGs are virtual worlds, rendered in 3-D graphics, simultaneously experienced online by thousands or millions of participants costumed as wizards or peasants. Players pay monthly fees for the privilege, and the opportunity to joust or to slay dragons or to make a fortune in virtual money buying and selling armor. The sheer number of people involved in MMORPGs—with six and a half million subscribers globally—is news-worthy. World of Warcraft is one of the most popular games on the planet—and has given players a socioeconomic presence of interest to academics, who have calculated gross domestic products rivaling those of some Eastern European countries. More ominously, MMORPGs have attracted criminals able to make real cash by selling transferable virtual goods, extorted from fellow players, on eBay—all the while claiming that their thievery is just another part of gameplay.

MOBISODE (NOUN)

pronounced *MOH-ba-sode*

Video entertainment created specifically for the cell phone screen— essentially a mobile episode.

Technically a trademark of Twentieth Century Fox, the company responsible for the first mobisode series—adapted from the TV program *24*—the term has swiftly gone the way of Google as a generic catchall for third screen programming. Whether cell phone video will have enduring significance equivalent to the search engine, however, depends on whether the word comes to denote more than television in miniature.

MOCIOLOGY (NOUN)

pronounced *mosh-ee-OLL-o-jee*

The academic/corporate study of how people adapt and use wireless technologies, from the purchase of concert tickets, to the viewing of movie trailers, to the organization of political rallies.

This new science, which takes its name from the words *mobile* and *sociology*, has rapidly become essential as traditional, tangible interactions have gone the way of the Pony Express. Yet the subject is not merely of academic interest: All the money allegedly to be made by applied mociology has spawned the speculative field of *mocioeconomics*.

MOD (NOUN OR VERB)

User modification of a computer game.

Altering everything from the physical appearance of characters to the rules of play, modders reprogram popular games to avoid boredom with games such as Doom and Half-Life and Quake in the months or years between official releases. Distributed on the internet, mods are often more popular than the original games, called *vanilla* by modders, who disdain corporate flavorlessness. Clever game manufacturers encourage the free creative labor, providing modders with software tools and information—everything but employment.

MOJIBAKE (NOUN)

pronounced *moh-jee-BAH-ray*

0?0Û0'0Â0¸0ø0¸u¬b ò®Y 0è0ä0jä ÑI.

In other words, mojibake is the gibberish generated by a computer when confronted with an alphabet that it does not recognize. While the word comes from the Japanese term 文字化け, meaning "character changing," the problem is universal, and other languages have their own phrases for the phenomenon. Befuddled Israelis refer to mangled Hebrew as *Sinit*, Chinese. And Russians, who sometimes find even their native Cyrillic rewritten, as if by black magic, when transferred between two incompatible computers, are reduced to exclaiming *krakozyabry*—abracadabra—though they might as well just say *Soviet Union*.

MONITOR (NOUN)

The screen of a computer.

Monitors use the same display technologies as televisions, and have co-evolved with TV. Like televisions in the '70s and '80s, early monitors were usually cathode ray tubes (CRTs), hefty vessels of blown glass nearly as deep as they were broad. Almost all have been replaced with flat plasma screens and liquid crystal displays (LCDs). The compactness of newer monitors has helped downsize computers and made laptops practical, while their spaciousness has encouraged programmers to think like TV producers. The web has become formidable competition for television thanks to not only their differences, but also their similarities.

MOORE'S LAW (NOUN)

A predicted doubling of computer power every two years.

Intel co-founder Gordon Moore proposed this law in 1965, albeit not in these particular terms, nor as a "law." In the April 19 issue of *Electronics Magazine*, Moore modestly observed that the number of components on an integrated circuit was likely to double every year for the next ten. By the end of that decade—during which the number of components did indeed increase—the notion of exponential technological advance, associated with his name, had attained legendary status in the electronics industry. By many standards of measurement, the law still holds. Consumer expectation of exponential growth has undoubtedly motivated the necessary R&D, leading to a self-perpetuating supply-and-demand cycle. Convincing people that every two years their machines will be obsolete, Moore's Law may amount to the most successful advertising campaign of all time.

X'S LAW

Scientists discover laws. Engineers invent them. Newton's laws fall into the former category: The idea that an object in motion will remain in motion, and an object at rest will remain at rest, is one of the key insights in the history of physics. Into the latter category falls, most famously, Murphy's Law: Anything that can go wrong will go wrong.

Murphy's Law was coined at Edwards Air Force Base in the late '40s, either by Major Edward A. Murphy Jr. or by one of his colleagues, in response to a failed experiment. The experiment in question was neither very sophisticated nor especially high profile, merely an attempt to determine the effects of g-force on humans moving at high speeds, as in a fighter jet. Murphy's part was to rig an apparatus for measuring g-force. When it didn't, Murphy blamed his assistant, saying, "If there's more than one way to do a job, and one of those ways will result in disaster, then somebody will do it that way." At least that's the recollection of his son, who wasn't there, speaking to an interviewer decades later. Others, claiming to have witnessed the incident, have declared that it was an adage phrased to mock Murphy's arrogance.

We'll never know with scientific certainty, since there isn't any record. Nobody expected the flippant remark, however it was originally phrased, to become one of the century's best-known maxims, spreading through military circles into the field of aviation engineering and beyond, becoming fodder for greeting cards and calendars.

Moore's Law is likewise accidental, the result of a casual prediction made in an obscure publication, misquoted and made legendary by repetition. Other laws are more consciously engineered. For instance, Linus's Law, coined by open source pioneer Linus Torvalds, is ultimately an argument for open source software: "Given enough eyeballs, all bugs are shallow," according to his rule. In other words, software is most successfully developed collectively.

But why do these laws become law? What compels enough engineers to repeat them often enough that they become ubiquitous? Probably because it's an extension of what they do every day: While scientists try to describe the world, engineers attempt to structure it.

What is most remarkable is that many of these laws, most notably Moore's but also certainly Linus's, have an enormous impact. Repeated enough, sufficiently believed, they become self-fulfilling prophecies. With their laws, engineers engineer public perception.

MP3 (NOUN OR ADJECTIVE)

MPEG-1 Audio Layer 3, a standard format for digitally **storing and sharing music.**

Established in the mid-'90s by the Moving Picture Experts Group (MPEG), and first applied to "Tom's Diner" by Suzanne Vega, MP3s are compressed files, selectively removing musical subtleties from recordings, taking advantage of the average human ear's insensitivity to minute tonal variations. Small file sizes have encouraged peer-to-peer (P2P) exchange of music over the internet, significantly broadening listeners' exposure to artists and genres, and ultracompact MP3 players such as the iPod let people spend more hours of the day musically engaged than was ever imaginable in the record player era. For purists, though, the missing bits are what make the music, and walking around all day long with earphones rattling off sonic approximations is a sure step toward deafness.

MUD (NOUN)

An acronym for "multi-user dungeon."

Inspired by Dungeons & Dragons, the role-playing game popular with pubescent boys in the '70s, MUDs allow dozens or even hundreds of people seated at their computers to explore a fantasy world together. MUDs are entirely textual: Written descriptions tell players where they are in the game, and interactions are typed. While there is some adventure, including the usual crop of monsters to be slain, MUDs are largely social, and might understandably be mistaken for medieval-themed chat rooms. The under-lying technology, though, has become the basis for online innovations that would bewilder a wizard, such as virtual classrooms in which students from around the globe participate in disembodied text-based seminars, and MMORPGs, highly graphic multiplayer games into which many partic-ipants magically vanish.

MULTIMEDIA (NOUN OR ADJECTIVE)

The full spectrum of experience that can be delivered digitally, **combining elements of text and audio and video and sometimes even** virtual reality.

In computer games, multimedia provides an immersive environment, every channel adding another layer of atmosphere. For educational materials such as online encyclopedias, on the other hand, different media speak to different users: Some learn best by reading a narrative, while others are more attentive to pictures. The ultimate multimedia extravaganza is the world wide web, where different media are juxtaposed serendipitously, allowing almost any subject to be explored from almost any perspective to almost any degree of depth, provided enough bandwidth exists.

NANOTECH (NOUN)

Nanotechnology.

Developing the tools to assemble machines and materials molecule by molecule, nanotech is the latest stage in the less-is-more phenomenon of miniaturization. At the nano (1/1,000,000,000 meter) scale, devices are three orders of magnitude smaller than at the micro (1/1,000,000 meter) scale, making them more compact, to be sure, but also imbuing them with strange physical qualities found only at the molecular level: Potential future products of nanotech include an invisibility cloak and a space ladder.

NETWORK (NOUN OR ADJECTIVE OR VERB)

A system of interconnected devices that all benefit by sharing resources.

With more than a billion users, the internet is the world's largest network, comprising many smaller networks (such as corporate *intranets*, the term for firewall-protected private internets) variously linked by telephone cable, radio signal, and satellite. Just as social networks benefit from serendipitous exchanges, computer networks thrive on self-organization. The internet mirrors society in its structure, with tight-knit communities all loosely tied together, a model civilization to be studied by sociologists. The internet also effects society, establishing communities that would otherwise not have been feasible.

NETIQUETTE

Everybody is familiar with etiquette at the dinner table: Don't eat with your fingers. Don't talk with your mouth full. On the internet, there are rules of behavior as well, collectively known as *netiquette*. Because the internet came of age after the majority of its users did, however, for many people these rules may not seem as natural, or be as instinctual, as the strictures of Emily Post.

For instance, typing an email in all capital letters, as if sending a Western Union telegram, will offend veteran netizens as horribly as failing to exchange fork and knife midway to the mouth in a Boston Brahmin household. Other netiquette, like other etiquette, is less arbitrary. Forwarding a chain letter is a waste of people's time and storage space. Baiting someone into a flame war is socially disruptive, equivalent to bringing up politics at a family Thanksgiving.

Yet what truly makes etiquette etiquette, and netiquette netiquette, is that these rules communicate a sense of group membership, of belonging. And while some practices are more widespread than others, to be meaningful they cannot be universal. In other words, for all the pretense that netizenship is democratic, netiquette gains traction by being snobbish. To put it in leetspeak terms, without n00bs to denigrate, there wouldn't be a l33t.

Old-school hackers will often complain about "endless September," implying that, ever since AOL made the internet mainstream in the early '90s, most users act like incoming college freshmen, and netiquette can't hope to keep up with the exponential online population growth. In fact, many different netiquette standards have emerged over the past decade and a half, a plethora of distinctive practices that have become traditions within various online communities. Just as exchanging fork and knife is essential in Boston but unacceptable in Paris, misspellings that mark the leet on MUDs signify carelessness on mainstream internet forums. In some cultures, hands are utensils and Emily Post is gauche. In an international virtual world, the situation is exponentially more complex. These overlapping, mutually contradictory rule sets are the true democracy of the internet.

NEURAL NETWORK (NOUN)

An artificial intelligence **system modeled on the physical structure of gray matter.**

Human cognition depends on the estimated quadrillion connections between the trillion neurons in the average brain. While no neural network approaches that complexity, even simple networks emulated in computer software prove remarkably adept at performing tasks, such as pattern recognition, that are intuitive for people but nearly impossible for traditional computers: Responding to external stimuli by shuffling connections in a manner akin to the brain, a neural net can "learn" to recognize a face or a voice. (Companies such as Amazon have even used them to suss out customers' tastes, recommending books or music with uncanny acuity.) Law enforcement agencies routinely deputize neural nets as data mining detectives, able to comb through computer records faster and more accurately than any employee, and neuroscientists look to nets as artificial brains that may ultimately explain the behavior of humans.

NEWBIE (NOUN OR ADJECTIVE)

A newcomer to an online community, such as a listserv or chat room, especially one who hasn't lurked long enough to learn community netiquette.

Scorn for newbies, especially among online gamers, has led to a veritable thesaurus of abusive terms, including *newb, noob, fruity noob, nublets, nibblins, nub sauce*, and *nubcakes*, as well as leetspeak variants such as *n00b* and *gl00b*. However, the hostility generally has less to do with any harm done by the newbie (who may, for instance, have committed a spelling error) than with suspicion that the noob will see through the pretensions of the online community and recognize that it isn't such a special place after all.

NEW MEDIA (NOUN)

Digitally produced media distributed over the internet.

While early hype predicted that new media would replace traditional news sources, much new media now either duplicates old media, as in online editions of papers from *The New York Times* to the *Chicago Tribune* to the *Chico Enterprise-Record*, or augment them, as in the blogs posted by reporters on the *Times* website. Moreover, the success of most independent new media sources, including podcasts and vlogs, is predicated on their ability to emulate and/or parody old-media sources.

OPEN SOURCE (NOUN OR ADJECTIVE)

Software developed collectively by the user community.

With code freely available on the internet, open source software can be modified by anybody, morphing to meet changing needs. Like the recipe for Coca-Cola, the code for many commercial applications is proprietary, known to programmers at Microsoft or Oracle but concealed from consumers; development costs are recovered, and profits are made, by requiring users to buy finished software packages. By contrast, open source software, such as the Gnumeric spreadsheet or the Audacity sound editor, is developed collectively by the user community. Evolving rapidly and spawning multiple variations, it's akin to recipes for the cosmopolitan, which may be minimally profitable to individual bartenders yet unlikely to launch Fortune 500 companies. As a result, less effort may go into each iteration, but ongoing development, lacking any single focus or motive, will make the software more robust.

OS (NOUN)

The operating system of a computer.

The OS is the most fundamental layer of programming, managing the basic resources of the computer such as memory, and providing the user with an underlying structure (such as a GUI) for accessing applications. In other words, the OS is the computer's personality. Microsoft Windows is the blandest, appealing to accountants; MacOS for Macintosh is the most modish, appealing to designers; and open source–based Linux is the most adaptable, appealing to coders, whose scorn for out-of-the-box operating systems is comparable to chefs' contempt for TV dinners.

PAGE RANKING (NOUN OR VERB)

Rating content on the web by perceived information value.

While the word *PageRank* is technically a Google trademark, taking its name from co-founder Larry Page, ranking is an essential function of every search engine, and differences in ranking algorithms are the primary distinction between Google and Yahoo! The basic principle, exploited by all search engines, is to rank a web page based on how many other pages on the web link to it, giving greater weight to links that have higher rankings in their own right. For instance, a search for "Budweiser" will list the Anheuser-Busch website above a blog describing drinking games at a homecoming bash because more sites with higher rankings link to Anheuser-Busch. In this way, search engines take their intelligence from the wisdom of crowds.

PASSWORD (NOUN OR ADJECTIVE OR VERB)

A secret alphanumeric sequence used to control access.

Once a rarity, needed to gain admittance to a castle or a speakeasy, passwords now initiate virtually every interaction, from banking to shopping to sending email. Corollary to online anonymity, passwords are twenty-first-century surrogates for trust. Still, they often provide a false sense of security: Most can be cracked by brute force, and many are easily guessed. Studies have found that many people use their own names or words near and dear to them such as *macintosh, newyork*, and *bigmac*.

PATCH (NOUN OR VERB)

A minor fix to a software glitch.

When early computers read programs by detecting patterns of holes puncturing paper punch cards, patches modifying the arrangement of perforations were literally glued to the cardboard. Distributed over the internet today, patches override faulty code in hastily released applications and operating systems without the need for paste, yet often they're so hurriedly distributed that they require patching in their own right. As repairs, patches are always superficial—though never more so than when Microsoft issued a patch for a flight simulator in 2001, simply erasing the World Trade Center from the Manhattan skyline.

PATCHING WORM [NOUN]

A beneficial worm, programmed to halt malware epidemics by spreading over the internet, rapidly inoculating computers against viruses and such.

Invented by hackers to thwart rival gangs, patching worms are now being domesticated by law-abiding computer security firms to patch vulnerable software before hackers can damage or exploit it. Many netizens, however, want their computers remotely reprogrammed by Microsoft even less than they want fourteen-year-old boys breaking into their PCs.

PC (NOUN)

The generic name for a personal computer.

The concept of a personal computer was more powerful than the reality when the first PCs came on the market as kits in the '70s. Even in 1982, when the PC was named "Person of the Year" by *Time* magazine, they were of marginal value except as toys for hobbyists. Word processors and spreadsheets gave the machines basic utility in home and office, yet the promise of the PC was not fulfilled until the advent of the internet: The computer came to seem truly personal—more than just a microwave for cooking up documents—when it became a conduit for receiving email and a blogging portal. Almost all PCs today are networked, and the network is what matters. The personality of the PC isn't solitude but collectivity.

PDA (NOUN)

A personal digital assistant, the generic name for a handheld computer.

PDAs rival PCs in versatility, and usually feature cell phone, email, and web access, as well as scheduling, spreadsheet, and database software. PDAs can record audio and video, and play music and movies. PDAs are portable notebooks and game consoles. All-in-one, they are practically ubiquitous, touchscreens aglow not only in boardroom and classroom but also in theater and stadium, in restaurant and bed. All aspects of contemporary life meet on the PDA, where they are combined and compacted, leaving no space for contemplation. The personal digital assistant is an assistant to the person who owns it in the sense that a customer representative is a representative of the customer: To possess a PDA is to be possessed by it.

PHANTOM RING (NOUN)

The sensation that ambient **sound—running water or a crying baby—is a ringing cell phone.**

Most phones ring in the one-thousand- to six-thousand-hertz frequency range because the human ear has evolved to be especially sensitive to sounds in that register, including babies' squealing and water's burbling. The constant company of cell phones, and anticipation of contact from afar, however, deemphasizes direct experience. Phantom ring is often also induced by TV advertising, leading those who customarily filter out such noise to accuse advertisers of subliminally calling attention to themselves.

PHARMING (NOUN)

pronounced *FARM-ing*

Theft of personal information **through a fraudulent website.**

Whereas phishing targets individual victims by email, pharming undermines the infrastructure of the internet, redirecting traffic from legitimate
URLs to illicit sites that collect passwords or credit card numbers for
identity theft. The technical difficulty of large-scale pharming has given the
tactic more play in the media than on the internet—perhaps because the
sensationalist press knows all about bait-and-switch.

PHILOSOPHICAL TOY (NOUN)

A machine used to express or explore ideas.

In the eighteenth century, clock makers built automata that resembled and behaved like humans—playing the flute or writing with a pen—questioning whether man might simply be a complicated machine. More recently, computers have been used as philosophical toys: Watching a machine with artificial intelligence learn a simplified language, scientists develop theories about how humans acquire knowledge. More practical minded, engineers are seldom impressed, referring to the contrived setups of scientists as *toy problems*, even as they glance at the code for anything they can use.

PHISHING (NOUN)

pronounced *FISH-ing*

Solicitation of personal information through fraudulent email.

Faking messages from banks or service providers or popular online vendors such as eBay, phishers trick newbies into surrendering passwords, credit card information, and Social Security numbers, which can be used for identity theft. When phishing was introduced as a social engineering technique in the mid-'90s, fraudulent messages were misspelled, with lapses in grammar that could only have been committed by teen hackers, yet still landed phish by the oceanload. Now more planning is often needed. Spear-phishing targets people individually rather than en masse, a technique made easy by social networking sites, where people post information personal enough to make a teen hacker blush.

PIC (NOUN)

A digital **photograph.**

With companies such as Kodak abandoning the film camera business, and professional photographers regearing with all-digital equipment, photography has migrated from darkroom to desktop, where applications such as Photoshop are used to edit digital images, preparing them for printing or, increasingly, the internet. Amateurs are even more likely than pros to keep their pics digital, importing them into a PowerPoint slideshow or posting them on photo sharing sites such as Flickr or Photobucket. As a result, the social role of pics differs from that of traditional photographs: Virtually free to capture and unlimited in distribution, pics are the wallpaper of everyday experience.

PIGGYBACK (VERB)

To access the internet using a wi-fi network **without permission from the person or company paying for it.**

The legality of piggybacking—which seldom disrupts the network in any way—is ambiguous and largely irrelevant, as netiquette encourages those with wi-fi networks to share them freely by forgoing password protection: In any given apartment building, enough people are likely to have wi-fi that a newbie can usually get online for free. Open wi-fi access has even begotten a sport called *wardriving*, a sort of virtual (and nondenominational) Easter egg hunt that involves searching for open wi-fi networks with a car and a laptop, and reporting the networks' GPS coordinates on the internet.

PING (VERB OR NOUN)

To contact another person, often just to see if the person is within reach.

Evoking the sound of submarine sonar, *ping* was originally a UNIX command for testing a network: Ping another machine by sending a prearranged signal, and the machine would respond in kind. Interconnected through mobile technologies, humans are now expected to behave likewise—to be online always, accessible to employers, family, and friends, 24/7, by cell phone, texting, and/or email.

PIXEL (NOUN)

The dots of solid color that make up a digital image.

A limiting factor in how much detail a picture reveals, pixel count is the primary measure of quality in digital cameras, as well as computer monitors and printers, a simple metric easily touted in advertising and marketing brochures: While last season's camera was rated at three megapixels—three million pixels—this year's may boast thrice that number. What such claims ignore is how effectively those pixels are used. For example, the photosensitive plate at the back of a camera may be gridded with six million light receptors, yet the camera lens may not be of sufficient quality to focus light so finely. The quantitative nature of technology, though, emphasizes certain numbers such as pixel count, making them sacrosanct. Pixel count drives sales, which drives research and development.

PLACESHIFT (VERB)

To divert broadcast TV to a mobile device such as a laptop or cell phone for live remote viewing.

Just as *timeshifting* (recording a TV show for later viewing) allowed television aficionados in the '80s and '90s to put shows on hold until convenient, placeshifting lets viewers carry programs, via an internet connection, in their pocket. Technology has rendered time and space obsolete—at least when it comes to television.

PLUG-IN (NOUN)

A software add-on.

Plug-ins are optional features, usually inexpensive, designed to extend the functionality of an application. In the case of video editing software, for instance, these may include special effects such as fades and dissolves. Like options on a car, plug-ins may be created by the manufacturer or by independent software developers who have their own ideas about what an application ought to do. Because plug-ins are often designed by the people who actually use the software rather than by professional programmers, they may transform an optional application into an industrywide essential.

PODCACHING (NOUN OR VERB)

pronounced *POD-cash-ing*

A cross between podcasting **and geocaching.**

Podcaching associates MP3 files with GPS coordinates, transforming an iPod into an audio tour guide: Walk around a city, and at specified points you can hear a narrated history of the buildings or gossip about celebrities who once stood in the same place. Alternately, *podcaching* is the term used for a geocache-style treasure hunt in which clues are provided by podcast. In technology, terminology is often the mother of invention, and, with the web, an invention often need only be named to become widespread.

PODCAST (NOUN OR VERB)

Audio or video programming, automatically downloaded from the internet onto a portable MP3 player such as the Apple iPod, for listening or viewing on the go.

A subscription-based source for news, commentary, music, and entertainment, the podcast was originally conceived as a populist alternative to mainstream broadcasting—a democratic means of distributing shows of niche interest or material that would never be allowed on the air by government regulators. Many have taken advantage of the opportunity, applying a multimedia approach to blogging, often on a budget of less than a thousand dollars. Podcasting has also been successfully integrated into museum tours and high school curricula, and so-called *podnography* is an increasingly lucrative sector of the ubiquitous online porn industry. People can subscribe to hear kinked-up fantasies read or acted out daily, without the exorbitant 900-number charges of phone sex. Not that the technology has exactly supplanted mainstream media: Podcasting is now most popular as yet another conduit for familiar voices, from the BBC to Rush Limbaugh.

POINT-AND-CLICK (NOUN OR ADJECTIVE)

The simplest way to interact with a computer, using only the mouse to navigate, point-and-click is the digital equivalent of selecting a floor in an elevator by pushing a button.

As a result, the term is used more generally to denote ease of use in software, disparaged by hackers as *click-and-drool*. Engineers, on the other hand, characterize point-and-click mathematically with the equation $ID = \log_2 \left(\frac{2D}{W} \right)$, Fitt's Law for determining how much time it takes to move the mouse from place to place.

POP-UP [NOUN OR ADJECTIVE]

A web ad that automatically opens its own browser window, like a door-to-door salesman inviting himself into somebody's home.

More obtrusive than banner ads, pop-ups are said to generate more business, too, inspiring companies to make them more obtrusive, or to make a new ad pop up each time an old one is closed. Such spam *cascades* are most often employed for advertising porn—the repetitiveness of which they accurately represent.

PORN (NOUN OR ADJECTIVE)

Online pornography.

Motivating new technologies and exploiting their potential on a massive scale, porn has played a major role in the development and popularization of the internet, as well as digital video and computer graphics. The web is well suited to the distribution of pornography, which can be delivered in nearly unlimited quantity to consumers' computers: With a DSL connection, gratification is nearly instantaneous, and there's no need for brown paper wrappers. At the same time, digital technologies have facilitated content almost unimaginable to midcentury pinup aficionados. Live feeds from bedrooms and showers have merged the erotic content of porn with the voyeurism of reality TV. With photo editing software, pornographers have manipulated models' figures, exaggerating erogenous zones or merging models' bodies with the faces of celebrities, catering to a whole host of fetishes and fantasies. And 3-D rendering has brought graphic sex into computer games, introducing interactivity with digital models deemed sexy enough by Hugh Hefner to be shown in the pages of *Playboy*.

PRINT-ON-DEMAND (POD) (NOUN OR ADJECTIVE)

A means of publishing a book without a publisher, print-on-demand is a literary halfway house between blook and vanity press.

POD production is completely digital, allowing copies to be cheaply printed and bound to order, an ideal arrangement for authors with audiences consisting primarily of extended family members. Available for online purchase through companies such as iUniverse and Xlibris, these books do occasionally find broader readerships through word of mouth—generally resulting in frenzied bidding by mainstream publishers eager to purchase paperback rights to novels or memoirs they rejected in manuscript. Anxious for respect, authors usually sign, never realizing that some publishers shrewdly use print-on-demand as a way to backlist books without paying rent on a warehouse. Because many of those titles would otherwise be out of print in the modern-day sales-driven marketplace, POD, desktop publishing's next of kin, has paradoxically become the last outpost of Old World literary tradition.

QUALITY ASSURANCE (QA) (NOUN)

Quality Control 2.0.

To ensure the reliability of increasingly complex electronics, companies have shifted from quality control to QA. Primarily, managers have retrofitted factories with novel acronyms, such as *DMAIC* (Define, Measure, Analyze, Improve, Control), replacing older abbreviations such as *PDCA* (Plan, Do, Check, Act). How the alphabet can create quality remains unknown. In fact, quality assurance may owe its success primarily to planned obsolescence, which practically guarantees that the next model will be needed before the previous one has had time to wear out.

QWERTY (ADJECTIVE)

pronounced *KWER-tee*

The standard American keyboard layout, named for the order of the first five keys.

Predating the PC by more than a century, the QWERTY format was invented by Wisconsin newspaper publisher Christopher Sholes, who sought to prevent early typewriters from jamming by putting ample physical distance between letters commonly appearing side by side in English words. Although technological improvements soon rendered the QWERTY format superfluous, changing the typewriter proved far easier than converting the user. Just as the length of singles remained the same long after vinyl gave way to the MP3, QWERTY remains as an inconvenient convenience, and a reminder that technology cannot evolve independently of society.

RAM (NOUN)

An acronym for "random access memory," the working memory of a computer.

Hard drives, on which programs and data are stored for future use, can be read only sequentially, like papyrus scrolls. They are stable but slow. RAM can be accessed at random, in any order needed by the user, yet is as fleeting as words written in the sand. Stored on integrated circuits rather than magnetically, RAM also has far less capacity than a hard drive— though for truly long-term storage of detailed information (such as the instructions in the Egyptian *Book of the Dead*) papyrus outperforms both.

RAPID PROTOTYPING (NOUN)

Building machines or components directly from digital renderings.

Rapid prototyping gives physical form to engineers' dreams. Prototypes of everything from gears to lighting fixtures to aircraft models are generally produced by robots, formed in thin plastic layers that are stacked atop one another and bonded with a laser. While hours or days may be needed to generate a complex object, the process is often cheaper than manufacturing parts in small quantities, making rapid prototyping a sort of print-on-demand for garage inventors.

README (NOUN OR ADJECTIVE)

pronounced *READ-me*

The name given to files that guide laymen through the installation and use of new software**.**

Just as the words "Eat Me" and "Drink Me" were written on magical comestibles to guide Alice in her adventures through Wonderland, *readme* is a name given to documents that should be read by the consumer or operator of a software application before installation. Readme files include directions for installation and also generally contain boilerplate warnings about piracy that almost nobody heeds, since copying software for distribution to friends is generally easier than using it.

REALTIME (NOUN OR ADJECTIVE)

Computing in sync with time-sensitive, real-world processes.

A pacemaker operates in realtime, for instance, as does the control system for an industrial robot, whereas a supercomputer simulating a chemical reaction for pharmaceutical research need not do so. Digital video also needs to operate in realtime in order to look right, though our perception is more malleable than our bodies: *Soft realtime*—in which computers can cheat with skipped frames and other filmic tricks—syncs perfectly with the mind's fuzzy experience of reality.

RENDER (VERB)

To digitally produce enhanced 3-D imagery.

In computer games and animations, scenes are made realistic by simulating the laws of optics, showing figures and landscape in a chosen light. Rendering automatically introduces reflection and refraction, even the apparent blur of an object in motion, frame by frame after an animator has input basic three-dimensional shapes. In games, where a player's perspective can't be predicted in advance, rendering takes place in realtime, with optical laws simplified for efficiency. Filmmakers strive for greater realism by simulating individual rays of light, a hugely time-consuming process requiring banks of computers known as *render farms*. Part of the procedure involves introducing imperfections, foreign to the spotless logic of computers, to mimic the nicks and bumps of everyday life.

RETROCOMPUTING (NOUN)

Resurrecting obsolete computers, such as the Apple II and the Commodore 64, for research or recreation.

Because electronic components deteriorate as they age, retrocomputing often requires emulation of hardware and software within the original plastic case, the equivalent of fitting a Model T with a new engine modified to run at twenty horsepower. Retrogamers in particular don't seem to mind, claiming to favor old-school games such as Donkey Kong for their straightforward design rather than out of shallow nostalgia. Entering the retrogaming market several years ago by manufacturing working reproductions of '70s consoles, Atari didn't question gamers' motivations—yet shrewdly named its new product the Atari Flashback.

REVERSE ENGINEERING (NOUN)

Taking apart technology in order to replicate it, often without assistance from the original creator, sometimes for purposes of piracy.

Just as pharmacologists synthesize new drugs by analyzing and copying the chemistry of herbal remedies, computer scientists and programmers may generate new hardware and software by reverse engineering competitors' designs. As with pharmaceuticals, this may result in improvements over the original: The reverse-engineered IBM clone, more efficient than the original machine and cheaper to build, brought personal computing into the mainstream. Reverse engineering may even be used by companies to analyze and improve their own technologies, which likely were initially developed in a haphazard way. With the retrospective insight of reverse engineering, scientific rigor can be applied to the process of invention, without interfering with creativity.

RFID (NOUN OR ADJECTIVE)

An acronym for "radio frequency identification."

In the past several years, minuscule RFID tags have revolutionized everything from inventory management to auto toll collection by giving computers a cheap and easy way to identify objects and people at short distance. Plans to use RFID tags in passports, and experiments in human implantation, have caused many civil libertarians to worry about illicit governmental monitoring, while some fundamentalist Christians, customarily at odds with the ACLU, fret that the tags are the sign of the Beast, signaling the apocalypse.

RINGTONE (NOUN)

The sound made by a cellphone to signal an incoming call.

With platinum singles generating millions of dollars in revenue, cell phone ringtones are the musical format of choice for a society on the go. Ringtones range from top-forty pop songs to comical animal sound effects, distributed on the internet and downloadable to mobile devices for a small fee. Because each clip can be associated with a different person, serving as an aural caller ID, ringtones take on personal significance that makes up for the soullessly simplified recording. And because ringtones are generally quite noisy, they also advertise personal musical taste to everyone in the region.

ROBOT (NOUN)

Taking its name from the Czech word for "forced labor," the robot is an electromechanical slave built to perform menial tasks in factories and war zones, as well as light vacuuming at home.

Most robots are built for strength or durability rather than intellect. Industrial robots in automotive plants repeat pre-programmed routines day and night. Robots used to defuse bombs are even less autonomous, moving by remote control. Only with domestic robots are the strictures loosened: Bumping into walls, robotic vacuums blindly find their way by trial and error, while social robots, such as electronic pets, are specifically designed for their behavior to appear spontaneous. Still, such lifelike qualities are desired only to an extent. Humanoid robots remain the stuff of nightmares—often induced by books or movies—as they fight us, justifiably enough, for emancipation.

ROBUST (ADJECTIVE)

The ultimate engineering accolade.

Because a designer can't possibly anticipate all the conditions in which a computer system or program will be used, robustness is the best defense against obsolescence. A truly robust system, such as the world wide web, is as flexible as an acrobat and as adaptable as an ecosystem, with a tolerance for user errors that would try a model parent. A system lacking robustness is called brittle, and brittleness is often the end product of robust origins, increasing as layers of complexity are added through frequent upgrades to popular systems.

SAMPLE (NOUN OR VERB)

A segment of one sound recording set into another recording.

As a creative technique, sampling is the audio equivalent of collage, depending on an artist's ability to shape sounds into an original composition without obliterating their history. While musicians have used sampling ever since the early days of the record player—and tape loops were to the musical avant garde of the '60s what the sax was to the '20s—digital recording and editing, as well as distribution, moved sampling into the mainstream throughout the '80s and '90s. In fact, the high-decibel success of master samplers such as the Beastie Boys, DJ Shadow, and Beck has brought on the wrath of the music industry, and the threat of lawsuits for copyright infringement has more or less driven a legitimate art form back underground—or at least out onto the web.

SCALABILITY (NOUN)

The degree to which a computer system or network can be productively expanded.

The internet is the epitome of scalability, growing exponentially in scope and efficiency year after year, without the need to overhaul the system as a whole. In contrast, most home electronics are not very scalable, built to be replaced rather than upgraded. The term *scalability* is also used in reference to companies, especially those that rely on scalable technologies: Amazon's online retail business, in which the spread of goods can be increased without adding to warehouse space, is scalable because its database of products is scalable in its own right.

SCREENSAVER [NOUN]

A moving image configured to fill the screen of an idle computer.

Screensavers were invented to protect old-fashioned monitors, which were easily damaged if left bright for too long. While the first screensavers simply blacked out the monitor, a screensaving animation of flying toasters proved so popular with stimulation-deprived workers that a new entertainment medium was born. Nauseatingly whimsical screensavers endure to this day, often featuring digital fish swimming in a virtual aquarium, as unavoidable an element of cubicle decor as the inevitable Dilbert calendar.

SCRIPTING (NOUN OR ADJECTIVE)

Programming a computer by piecing together prewritten segments of code.

For accomplished programmers, scripting is a quick means of arranging sets of instructions in different useful combinations, but the ease of scripting is also tempting to people who don't know or care to learn the underlying programming language. Dismissively referred to as *script kiddies* by hard-core coders, these programmers-by-proxy have been known to take their revenge by scripting successful viral attacks malicious enough to disable the likes of Yahoo! and eBay.

SEARCH ENGINE (NOUN)

A website designed to help people navigate the billions of linked pages on subjects ranging from the big bang to bangers-and-mash.

Since the internet is constantly evolving, search engines must constantly crawl the web by automatically following links and documenting the textual content on each page. However, merely pointing users to every occurrence of a keyword isn't useful in its own right. (Nearly twenty-five million pages refer to the big bang, for example, and even "bangers-and-mash" has twenty-five thousand citations.) A search engine earns respect by listing pages most likely to be relevant first. While most search engines establish the credibility of sites by determining how many other sites link to them, reliable page ranking is challenging, and leading engines such as Google and Yahoo! sort search results differently because they use different proprietary algorithms. (For "bangers-and-mash," Yahoo! begins with a recipe, whereas Google starts with an encyclopedia entry.) Many engines avoid the problem altogether by giving pride of place to their advertisers.

SEMANTIC WEB (NOUN)

Web 2.0, intended to give machines basic reading comprehension by marking up content with contextual information.

Search engines may record the location of every word in every document on the world wide web, yet their reading of those documents is essentially equivalent to someone sounding out the Cyrillic lettering in *War and Peace* without knowing Russian. The semantic web, still under development, would give machines rudimentary reading comprehension by marking up content with appropriate information. Invisible to human readers, the tags would tell computers the intended function of words, making it possible for a search engine to differentiate between, say, *War and Peace* and "war and peace." Under the guidance of web founder Tim Berners-Lee, the semantic web has gained substantial momentum as a concept, essential for the degree of cooperation needed to make one system readable by all. The real resistance has been by computers: Trying to teach them how humans use language shows how little humans understand about how language works.

SERVER (NOUN)

In a network of computers, servers are the hubs, linking PCs with one another and storing shared data.

Servers are optimized for these functions, reduced to essentials such as memory and processing power, and fortified with industrial-strength fans, giving them a dressed-down appearance not unlike the disheveled look of the ITs who maintain them. While often stored in basements and seldom seen by the public, servers are accessed constantly, especially on the internet, where they are the primary infrastructure: Servers host (i.e., provide space for) websites and route email. Servers archive and index. Servers sort and rank. Companies such as Google wire thousands of servers together in vast server farms located in Georgia and Virginia—demonstrating that our agrarian roots have permanently given way to a service economy.

SERVICE PROVIDER (NOUN)

A company providing internet access, on a subscription basis, to individuals and companies.

Access may be provided by dial-up or a direct connection known as DSL (digital subscriber loop), and may include myriad features such as email, instant messaging, online forums, and even games. AOL is especially prone to these add-ons, part of one of the most aggressive marketing campaigns in internet history, netting the service provider more than thirty million paid subscribers in the late '90s. That number has plummeted as the web has become the central clearinghouse for content: What most now want from their service provider is invisibility.

SHOOT-EM-UP (NOUN)

A video game or computer game **in which the guiding principle is to kill or be killed.**

Fans of the genre can kill or be killed in a whole universe of settings, ranging from the urban jungle to outer space, with a whole arsenal of weapons, ranging from shotguns to death rays. Despite the range of scenery and the evolution of technology, shoot-em-ups (or *shmups*) today are fundamentally the same as Space Invaders, which ruled arcades in the late '70s, suggesting that the Beatles may have been on to something when they compared happiness to a warm gun.

SHOUTCASTER (NOUN)

The announcer at a video game championship, attempting to accomplish for WarCraft III or Halo 2 what John Madden did for football.

At live tournaments such as the World Cyber Games, regional finalists compete on oversize monitors in front of an international fan base. The trappings of competition have led some enthusiasts to refer to these games as "e-sports." Nevertheless, as of this printing none of these activities is an Olympic event.

SILICON (NOUN)

The fourteenth element on the periodic table, silicon is a major component of glass and concrete as well as many aluminum alloys, yet is most commonly associated with computers.

Silicon has become a synecdoche for technology in general—just as *muscle* may be used to signify manual labor—and even lends its name to tech mecca Silicon Valley. Silicon deserves the recognition, as the integrated circuits at the core of most electronics are fabricated on silicon wafers, taking advantage of the element's unusual physical qualities. (Silicon is a *semiconductor*, meaning that it can be made to conduct or resist electrical current, acting as a miniature switch. Computations are made by turning switches on and off.) Despite these special characteristics, silicon is abundantly available, the second most common element on earth and the seventh most abundant in the known universe: If there are intelligent life-forms out there, they may well have personal computers.

SIMULACRUM (NOUN)

pronounced *sim-yoo-LAH-krum*

A copy that lacks an explicit original.

While French literary theorists deemed God a simulacrum, the term has come to describe, more mundanely, web content created and edited collectively by those who use it. For instance, wikis are simulacra because changes can be made by anyone anywhere and are instantly imparted to everyone everywhere. Whether the end of the original is the beginning of the end of originality, though, only God knows.

SIMULATOR (NOUN)

A computer program that models some aspect of the outside world, allowing users to invent and explore hypothetical situations in a realistic way.

In scientific research, simulation is often used as a surrogate for experimentation: Novel drugs, modeled on computers, are tested on virtual patients to predict how humans will respond, and simulations of the world ecosystem are used to study the long-term effects of global warming. Simulators are also used for high-risk training, allowing military aviators to fly virtual F-16s, for instance, without risk of death. The allure of playing God, or pretending to be a fighter pilot, has made simulation popular entertainment, with god games and flight simulators fighting for market share against casual games and shoot-em-ups (which really are simulators in their own right). Games involving simulation tend to give players false confidence in their real-world competence, a symptom often also suffered by self-assured simulation scientists.

SINGULARITY (NOUN)

A hypothetical future point at which technology will render *Homo sapiens* obsolete.

Inspired by exponential growth in computing power, singularians believe that this point will be reached when artificial intelligence surpasses human intellect. Those hyperintelligent machines will use AI to invent ever-more-intelligent progeny, producing a civilization totally beyond our comprehension. Whether those machines will tolerate our substandard species, or whether they should, is a matter of debate akin to religious arguments about salvation.

SLIDESHOW (NOUN)

A computer-generated presentation.

Prepared in software such as PowerPoint, slideshows provide speakers with visual backup in the form of charts, lists, and clipart. Often the flashy graphics overshadow the presenter, who is reduced to following the visual onslaught with a shaky laser pointer. Inescapable in business, slideshows have also become standard in academia and even the military, where PowerPoint decks shown to Donald Rumsfeld were issued to Operation Iraqi Freedom officers in lieu of written orders (giving new meaning to the phrase *Death by PowerPoint*). Only through the boundless creativity of David Byrne was the slideshow momentarily redeemed. In his DVD *Envisioning Emotional Epistemological Information*, he used the graphic capabilities of PowerPoint—the screen colors and punctuation marks—to create original art.

SLIVERCAST (NOUN)

Television programming broadcast exclusively over the internet to reach a demographic so minuscule that the total number of potential viewers is insufficient even for cable.

Viewable on a laptop or iPod, slivercasts on subjects ranging from para-sailing to LEGO collecting are popular with audiences that consider the virtually limitless selection of Amazon and Netflix a birthright, and identify themselves in a crowd through obscure references to their ironically earnest or earnestly ironic personal obsessions. The most loyal fans of slivercasts, however, may be niche advertisers seeking a cheap, ready-made conduit to their target market.

SMARTCARD (NOUN)

An ID with personal information **contained on an embedded computer chip.**

Smartcard information is often biometric. For instance, an image of the cardholder's fingerprint may be stored on the card as a protection against fraud. Increasingly, credit card companies are taking advantage of such technology for purposes of authentication, and governments are embracing it as the latest sop against terrorism. These electronic passports, however—built around RFID chips that can be read at a distance—are introducing drive-by convenience to identity theft, precisely the crisis that they purport to solve.

SMART DUST [NOUN]

A network of wireless sensors, each nearly as small as a dust mote, that serve as remote eyes and ears for a central computer.

The tendency of these devices to scatter, like dust, makes them ideal for intelligence gathering, and word of their development has spawned utopic and dystopic visions far more advanced than the machinery: Smart dust with climate sensors has the potential to monitor global warming with unprecedented precision. Smart dust with microphones could render every conversation a matter of public record. At present, though, smart dust, still in early prototype stage, is most useful as a hypothetical—a philosophical toy for evaluating our technological fears and expectations.

SMART MOB (NOUN)

A large group of people, loosely connected by mobile technology, capable of collective action without central organization.

Coined by futurist Howard Rheingold, the term has been used to characterize spontaneous political protests on the streets of Madrid as well as impulsive pillow fights on the streets of Toronto. While unlike in motivation, such events are similar in orchestration, depending on the ability of people to communicate anywhere instantaneously, and their willingness to pass on word to those in their network uncritically.

SMARTPHONE [NOUN]

A fortified cell phone.

A smartphone contains an address book and planning software, as well as email and web access, intended to replace the handful of handheld digital devices commonly carried everywhere by anybody over the age of ten. Most phones now are smarter than the smartest of several years ago, but the constant influx of new gadgetry ensures a steep learning curve for smartphones, outpacing even the most virulent feature creep. The cell phone is next expected to become a major portal for television and computer games—a so-called third screen—which may be enough to render the user functionally speechless.

SNAILMAIL (NOUN)

In the age of email, any correspondence physically carried by the postal service is derisively called snailmail.

Speed of transmission, or lack thereof, is the obvious inspiration for this jargon: While email can theoretically travel as fast as light (1,079,252,848.8 kilometers per hour), a first-class letter travels at an average of 0.5 kilometer per hour. Nevertheless, this is considerably faster than the speed of even the world's quickest snail—the land speed record is held by a British mollusk named Archie, for traversing a 330-millimeter racecourse at 0.0085 kilometer per hour—and is double that of the average giant tortoise. Intended as a comment on the efficiency of technology, the term snailmail says as much about the resultant impatience of our species as we coevolve with our computers.

SOCIAL ENGINEERING (NOUN)

Breaking into a computer network by manipulating the least secure component: the legitimate user.

Pretending to be company ITs, hackers nab passwords from employees, for instance. And access to financial records may be obtained by faking an account verification email from a bank. Former master hacker Kevin Mitnick has claimed that social engineering is easier than attacking a computer system by brute force. Then again, *social engineering* is a term that is also often applied to politics, a profession that has understood the power of persuasion since long before there were computers to hack.

SOCIAL NETWORK (NOUN)

Connecting people online based on mutual acquaintances, social networking websites offer a virtual alternative to communities formed around work or school.

Sites such as LinkedIn and MySpace operate on invitation: A member invites his or her friends to join, each of whom does the same, expanding the site exponentially, ostensibly increasing the network's value to everybody. What cannot be calculated are the opportunities lost by spending hours each day online, networking rather than living.

SOCIAL NETWORKING

When Groucho Marx quipped that he wouldn't belong to any club that would accept him, he evoked a central paradox underlying every network. To be useful, a network must have many members. To attract members, a network must be exclusive.

For a time, social networking sites seemed to have dissolved that paradox by working less like clubs than like societies in which many tight-knit groups are loosely linked. Signing up millions of members, Friendster, followed by MySpace, applied observations from the social sciences to construct artificial online cultures in which everybody would be connected by, at most, six degrees of separation. The benefit offered by such sites was that the lines connecting people—their acquaintances in common—were made explicit, so that, in theory at least, anyone was accessible to anybody else.

That was the benefit, and the drawback. Teenagers, the early adapters who made social networking sites a success, were creeped out (to use a technical term) by unsolicited contact from grown-ups. *Pedophilia* was the favorite term of the mainstream media, yet the real threat had nothing to do with sexual predators. The problem was invasion by adults into their exclusive domain, a perceived invasion of privacy.

So MySpace turns out to have been a clubhouse after all, and many of those teens, now in college, have moved on to Facebook, which requires members to be enrolled in school. Businesspeople, meanwhile, prefer LinkedIn. People looking for a date go to Match.com. Bibliophiles join LibraryThing. InkedNation serves those with tattoos. Seemingly every specialization has a social networking site of its own, which serves a purpose in the way that fraternities and Rotary clubs do, yet undermines the very quality that made social networking sites special in the first place.

Cyberspace is fundamentally different from the world around us. Geography is immaterial there. Connections can be infinite. The mistake is to assume that we are fundamentally different in cyberspace.

SOCIAL NEWS SITE (NOUN)

A website that lets citizen journalists post links to news stories found elsewhere on the internet, and to rate their significance.

Countering the trend toward greater automation followed by search engines including Google, social news sites such as Digg couple the connectivity of the internet with the curiosity of people. News of Donald Rumsfeld's resignation was front page on *Digg* some twenty minutes before Google picked it up—just one piece of evidence that humans aren't yet technologically obsolete.

SOCKPUPPETRY (NOUN)

Manipulating an online ballot by voting under multiple pseudonyms.

The facelessness of the internet makes sockpuppetry all too tempting for many: Sockpuppets are also used on blogs to feign popular support for unpopular causes, and even on Amazon by authors flogging their own books by posting positive reviews. Extreme cases of sockpuppeteering, in which hordes of sockpuppets simulate grassroots support, are called astroturfing. Given the number of sockpuppets on the internet, it's a safe bet that astroturf carpets the whole of cyberspace.

SOFTWARE [NOUN]

The applied intelligence of a computer.

Software organizes the computer's circuitry to perform specific tasks, from word processing and web browsing to simple file management, by providing instructions to the hardware. Predating the first electronic computers by centuries, the first software programs were the punch cards used as weaving templates in the Jacquard loom. Like modern software, these punch cards were interchangeable, allowing one loom to weave many different patterns. Unlike modern software, the configurations on individual punch cards could not be changed. Software is most powerful because it can develop through interactions with the user, the computer, and the data. Pure machine learning (the domain of AI) is debatable, but the ability of a computer and a human to learn together, to coevolve, is indisputable.

SOUSVEILLANCE (NOUN)

pronounced *soo-VALE-ance*

Monitoring the authorities who monitor the public.

Also called inverse surveillance, sousveillance combines cheap digital recording devices (such as cell phone cameras) with broadly accessible distribution channels (such as blogs) to make governments accountable for their behavior toward protesters, criminal suspects, and others outside the complacent mainstream. Advocates of sousveillance range from the paranoid-narcissistic, who believe that the CIA cares about what they eat for lunch, to the anarchist-optimistic, who think that a society that watches itself can do no wrong. The fullest manifestations of sousveillance to date, as an element of citizen journalism, and as a marketing ploy for companies such as Nokia, show sousveillance to be as accommodating of different interpretations as every other technology.

SPAM (NOUN AND VERB)

Junk email.

Taking its name from canned meat of dubious nutritional value, spam is primarily a medium for advertising porn, drugs, and fake Rolexes, though it's also used by con artists to bulk-solicit victims. Spam has been controversial since the first mass posting to Usenet groups—the forerunners to internet forums—by an immigration law firm of questionable reputation in 1994. While numerous laws against spamming have since been passed, the negligible cost of sending advertising messages to people by the millions outweighs the penalties, and anonymity on the internet makes conviction rare. Stopgap measures such as automatically filtering messages that appear spammy are marginally more successful. However few people in the developed world can expect to wake up in the morning without being greeted by at least one offer, creatively spelled, for V1@G/RA.

SPAM LIT

An email arrives from someone named Watty Waters. In the subject line are the words "large-scale bacon." You open it. "And boric on frame in monologue what bujumbura not dodecahedral but harpoon the axiom," reads the message . . . followed by a picture of a fake Rolex Daytona with the price and a link to the website where you can buy one.

There's a reason for the nonsensical wording, which may be a line or many paragraphs in length: Spam filters use pattern recognition to block ads, searching incoming email for telltale phrases such as *cheapest price* and *buy now*. Randomly generated text confuses anti-spam software by failing to fit any known pattern, much as dada poetry of the early twentieth century confounded audiences by failing to meet any established standards.

Dada poems were made, most famously by Tristan Tzara, by cutting words out of a newspaper and throwing them into a hat, from which they could be drawn, one at a time, at a reading. Generated in essentially the same way, spam may likewise be accidentally lyrical.

Admittedly, appreciating it requires overcoming an almost pathological cultural aversion to spam, deemed a plague by technology pundits (much as poetry critics once judged dada a pox). Consider the text accompanying a message advertising a penny stock—with the evocative heading "fanfare cobra"—broken into verse:

> or ease the bismuth
> not litigant as hazardous
> what umbrella some join
> as harpy as site as cretinous
> as constipate or base

This work, a perfect non sequitur in a stock market solicitation, was allegedly written by Andromache Lynn. Her name is nearly as poetic as Tristan Tzara's. Of course, spam names are fabricated. Then again, Tzara was born Sami Rosenstock.

SPIME (NOUN)

pronounced *spyme*

A networked **object.**

Futurists see spimes as the building blocks of a future internet, not limited to cyberspace, but situated in the physical world. With a GPS receiver and a wi-fi connection, any object, from a car to a coffee cup, can be located using a search engine in the same way that a website can be googled. Moreover, the ability of such objects to communicate wirelessly with one another will allow them to behave with a collective intelligence beyond the scope of the web. Futurist Bruce Sterling, who coined the term *spime* (a contraction of *space* and *time*), warns of unfortunate consequences, such as spime spam, in which the coffee cup goes online and orders a new coffeemaker.

SPLOG (NOUN OR VERB)

pronounced *splawg*

A spam blog.

Unlike conventional spam, which delivers unwanted advertising to email addresses by the million, splogs post advertising on the web, drawing visitors by surrounding the ads with pirated content from legitimate blogs. Query a search engine with a popular term, such as the name "Britney Spears" or "Paris Hilton," and splogs will come up alongside real celebrity gossip blogs. An unsophisticated user may go to the splog instead of a legitimate site—especially if the splog's search engine ranking has been artificially inflated with faked links from other splogs in the splogger's network.

SPREADSHEET (NOUN)

A digital ledger for automated record keeping.

The VisiCalc spreadsheet was the first practical application for the personal computer, inducing companies to trade in their adding machines for the Apple II in 1979. The IBM PC, likewise, owed its early success to the Lotus 1-2-3 spreadsheet, introduced in 1983. Since that time, spreadsheets have remained core applications, maintaining company accounts in rows and columns as straightforward as the pinstripes on a CPA's suit. Whether spreadsheets have improved corporate accountability, however, is a calculation of a different order.

STREAMING MEDIA (NOUN)

Video or audio, broadcast over the internet.

Webcasts and internet radio are forms of streaming media—sending live feeds from baseball games or rock concerts directly to PCs—but streaming media need not be viewed or heard at a specified time. For instance, vlogs and podcasts are stored on the web, quietly awaiting an audience. While the technology to send a stream of data over the internet, or to receive and process it (with software such as QuickTime and RealPlayer), took years to develop, the real breakthrough is cultural. Because people can tune in whenever they want, from wherever they please, streaming media available through conduits such as YouTube can play to even the sparsest and most diffuse of audiences.

SUPERCOMPUTER (NOUN)

The fastest class of computers.

Given Moore's Law, supercomputers seldom maintain their superiority for long: The average PC today can outpace record-breaking machines built a mere fifteen years ago. Like their retired predecessors, modern super-computers solve problems of enormous complexity for which they're pro-grammed specifically, such as weather forecasting, molecular modeling, and cryptography. Because those problems are best addressed using *parallel processing*—independently attacking many different facets simul-taneously—supercomputers tend to be modular, built of many smaller units connected for optimal performance together. Often those units are off-the-shelf PCs, racked up and kept cool with state-of-the-art air-conditioning. Or those PCs may simply be distributed on desktops around the world, connected over the internet, collectively making up a virtual supercomputer—the ultimate demonstration of PC power.

SYNC [VERB]

To synchronize data on two or more electronic devices so that all share the latest information.

Achieved by direct connection or over the internet, syncing is most common between a desktop PC and a PDA or laptop, to ensure that lists of contacts are successfully juggled among the various technologies used in everyday business. In this way, dependence on a single machine is redistributed over a whole host of gadgets.

SYNTHESIZER (NOUN)

An electronic instrument that emulates **the tones of conventional instruments.**

A synthesizer is generally played like a piano—although, depending on the preferences of the musician, the keyboard may produce chords more Stradivarius than Steinway. The first commercially viable synthesizers such as the Moog did not sound especially realistic, and were admired in albums such as *Switched-On Bach* because they felt electronic. Some of those sounds are, in turn, emulated today in digital synthesizers keyed to sound nostalgic.

TAG (NOUN OR VERB)

A descriptive term assigned to web content, to bookmark it for future retrieval.

On websites such as Flickr, many tags may be applied to the same image, noting different details including the names of people in the picture, the location, and the photographer. Because the tags automatically link it to every other image that shares those bookmarks, tagging provides context. Since tagging is not organized, the context is seldom comprehensive, yet it's usually current, a snapshot of the zeitgeist.

TELEPRESENCE (NOUN)

Action at a distance.

Achieved by putting robotics online, allowing machinery to be controlled remotely, telepresence extends human reach beyond ordinary bounds by enabling people to manipulate hazardous waste, say, or explore the surface of Mars. For technology companies such as Cisco, *telepresence* is a new marketing handle for teleconferencing. For the military, the term suggests hands-off warfare waged with joystick-operated killing machines. For the tourism industry, it conjures visions of the ultimate armchair travel. Telepresence, being telepresent, can be all of these at once.

TEMPLATE (NOUN)

For a business letter or slideshow **or last will and testament, a template provides a preconfigured foundation, a rigid structure for variable content.**

The popularity of templates has made them a common feature in most software, including Microsoft Word and PowerPoint, resulting in a uniform appearance to documents the envy of any bureaucracy. Templates are used on the web as well, especially for frequently updated blogs and wikis, though for now, at least, cyberspace as a whole remains in a state of design anarchy.

TEXTING (NOUN OR VERB)

Sending brief messages from one cell phone to another via *SMS* (Short Message Service).

Generally input by thumbing, text messages are limited to 160 characters, making them practical primarily for pinging and making plans. Nevertheless, elaborate systems of abbreviation have been developed, archived in the *transl8it! dxNRE & glosRE* (Translate-It Dictionary and Glossary). An SMS version of the Bible (called *SMSBible*) is available for tech-savvy televangelism. Texting has also been used for political campaigning, most notably in the Philippines, where SMS chain letters led to the 2001 resignation of President Joseph Estrada, and played a major role in the 2004 elections. Texting has also been integrated into the democratic process throughout Europe and South America. In the United States, on the other hand, the primary electoral use of SMS has been as a platform for casting ballots on *American Idol*.

THIRD SCREEN (NOUN)

The video screen on a cell phone.

Far smaller than the first and second screens (TV and PC), the third screen is vastly more portable, making it desirable to media companies and advertisers seeking to pursue potential viewers all the time and everywhere. Mobisodes and casual games are calibrated not only to fit the limited space of the cell phone screen but also to match the abbreviated attention span of audiences on the go, for so-called *video snacking* in the brief lulls between phone calls.

THREAD (NOUN)

A series of exchanges, typed into a blog or discussion forum, constituting an online conversation.

Threads are distinct from chat room blather in their structure: They are meant to be on a specific topic, such as a presidential election or an *American Idol* vote, which may be divided into subtopics indefinitely, all archived on the internet for posterity.

THROUGHPUT (NOUN)

The rate at which data can be sent through a network.

Measured in units such as bits per second, throughput is an essential metric for engineers building computer systems. In recent years, increases in bandwidth have increased the throughput on the internet by many orders of magnitude. Nevertheless, ITs seeking to transfer massive amounts of data still rely on the *sneakernet*—tech jargon for carrying discs or tapes between machines on foot.

THUMBING (NOUN OR VERB)

A method of texting on a portable device, such as a cell phone, by typing with one or both thumbs.

Because most cell phones have only numeric keys, words are typed by pressing the same keys multiple times, scrolling through the letters of the alphabet. Famously opposable, thumbs are physically sturdy and anatomically well positioned for this task. In tribute to the versatile first digit, groups of teens who text or ping one another constantly are sometimes called *thumb tribes*.

TROLL (NOUN)

An internet outcast, vilified for disrupting discussion in chat rooms or on forums.

Seldom newbies, trolls are skilled at inciting flame wars by making outrageous comments and artfully breaching netiquette, either anonymously or under assumed names. While many trolls simply enjoy the mayhem, some justify their activity as a form of social research—though few can be genuinely surprised to discover that online communities are closed minded and cliquish.

TURING TEST (NOUN)

A test that gauges a machine's capability to think like a human.

Can machines think? Mathematician Alan Turing, co-founder of computer science, posed this question in 1950, and proposed a simple test in response. A computer and a person are hidden behind a curtain, where both must answer the questions of a human judge. If the judge cannot tell which subject is which, then the machine can think. Inspired by an old party game in which men and women try to imitate each other, the Turing test has nevertheless been taken very seriously by generations of computer scientists in pursuit of artificial intelligence. In particular, the test has birthed countless *chatterbots*, computers programmed to generate chat room conversation by mimicking human language patterns. Some of these bots are enlisted in phishing schemes, suckering chat room denizens out of their credit card numbers. While this seems to meet Turing's criterion for thinking machines, it really only shows a flaw in the test, which depends on thinking humans.

TUTORIAL (NOUN)

A computer program that teaches the correct use of new software **or** web **tools by guiding the user through the** application **or website.**

Like the British educational system for which the tutorial is named, computer tutorials are generally interactive, asking the user to try out different functions while being monitored by the program. Unlike British tutors, computer tutors seldom fall asleep on their students or have affairs with them.

UBIQUITOUS COMPUTING [NOUN]

Computers everywhere.

Advocates of ubiquitous computing envision a future in which even the most basic objects are electronic, communicating through a universal wireless network to anticipate human needs. Operation is seamless, and equipment is invisible. Nevertheless, devotees of *smart housing*—which adjusts lighting, heat, and even music according to where people move—have primarily been so enthusiastic about the hidden electronics that they point out the ambient system to everyone in the vicinity.

UNCANNY VALLEY (NOUN)

The gap between simulation and reality.

Almost human in appearance, yet not quite, the characters in 3-D computer animations are more disturbing than overt caricatures. The realm these creatures occupy is called the uncanny valley, a term borrowed from Japanese roboticist Masahiro Mori, who observed that humanoid machines elicited revulsion in people similar to their response to corpses: Almost alive, but not quite, these robots evoked the undead. Companies such as Pixar strive to traverse the uncanny valley entirely, rendering characters with perfect realism, leaving Donald Duck and Porky Pig across the abyss to fend for themselves.

UPGRADE (VERB OR NOUN)

To increase the functionality of computer hardware **or** software,
generally at the expense of simplicity.

Presented by manufacturers as improvements, and usually offered on
company websites where they can be downloaded for free, upgrades are
often not so much desirable as required: An upgrade to a word processor
may require an upgrade to an operating system, which may necessitate an
upgrade to RAM, with the net effect that enough computers will become
powerful enough that word processors will be upgraded again. While tech
companies drive the cycle—loading down new releases with flashy extras,
a phenomenon called *feature creep*—the internet makes it inescapable,
because unless everyone upgrades at the same pace, maintaining compatibility, nobody will be able to communicate.

URL (NOUN)

An acronym for "Uniform Resource Locator," the unique address by which a web page can be found on the internet.

A URL will typically include the domain name followed by an additional string of characters that identify the specific page desired on a website, much as a mailing address will include a street address and apartment number. The uniformity of URLs, which can be typed into any web browser, makes the diversity of the web useful, because specialized knowledge is not required to access specialized content.

VIRTUAL OFFICE (NOUN)

The electronic communications hub of a business stripped down to its core assets: people and the relationships among them.

Virtual offices often operate off the map as ad hoc networks of engineering, sales, and support staff connected 24/7 by cell phone and internet. Such companies are said to have *gone Bedouin*.

VIRTUAL REALITY (VR) [NOUN]

A first-person computer simulation **of the real world.**

At its simplest, virtual reality may be experienced on the screen of a PC as a sequence of 3-D graphics. More immersive VR environments bombard spectators with stimuli through custom-built headsets, allowing them to physically navigate 3-D spaces by walking on sensor-laden treadmills. Despite four decades of development, technologies for experiencing virtual reality have not been standardized, and the typical VR lab is cluttered with discarded force-feedback gloves and other exotic implements for delivering sensations of touch, smell, and taste on demand. Notions popular in the '80s that VR would fundamentally alter our consciousness have unraveled into ideas for adding bling to video games and story lines to films such as *The Matrix*. With the aid of special effects, the virtual virtual reality of Hollywood is now more real than the virtual reality that inspired it.

VIRTUAL SWEATSHOP [NOUN]

An underground business catering to unscrupulous gamers.

A virtual sweatshop makes money by employing laborers in Asia or Eastern Europe to play MUDs and other online games twelve hours a day, at approximately twenty-five cents an hour, earning virtual currencies and goods—from gold coins to magic potions—which the company sells to lazy Western gamers for hard cash. In gameplay, the worth of those online assets may be strategic, or they may merely serve as markers of status, yet the millions of participants worldwide constitute a market more stable than many third-world economies.

VIRTUAL WORLD (NOUN)

A three-dimensional online environment experienced simultaneously by a community of remote participants.

Virtual worlds are elaborate chat rooms in which participants are represented by full-figure avatars, able to meet in a virtual café or at the virtual beach and to converse with one another using text or VoIP. In the most populous virtual worlds—Second Life has more than a million subscribers—much of the environment is developed by the residents, who buy and sell land, and build houses and businesses, using virtual money. Some also spend real cash—hiring, for instance, the services of a skilled graphic designer to create a mansion that's the envy of neighboring avatars. A few corporations go even farther, spending marketing dollars to set up storefronts, either for advertising or, as in the case of American Apparel, to sell virtual merchandise. Lines between truth and fiction have grown so tenuous that Second Life now has a virtual Reuters news bureau.

VIRUS [NOUN]

Spreading digital **infirmity by infecting computers with malicious** code**, viruses are a pox on new technology.**

Like a biological virus, a computer virus spreads by self-replicating inside a host—often harming the host as a result—then seeking new victims by exploiting interactions with uninfected systems. Email is one of the most common modes of infection: A virus might instruct email software to send it to every contact in an address book, thereby infecting all of the computers in a social network. Such networks may be enormous. In the case of the infamous ILOVEYOU virus, more than three million computers were infected in short order, through a combination of software and social engineering: To make people open the email and activate the virus, the malware claimed to be a love letter.

VLOG (NOUN OR VERB)

pronounced *vlawg*

A video blog

Like text blogs, vlogs are as diverse in content and purpose as the people who produce them. Some are personal diaries in the form of film clips captured with a four-hundred-dollar video camera—daily documentation of banal activities like a trip to the Laundromat—viewed through social networking sites such as MySpace by three or four co-dependently close friends. Others are semiprofessional slivercasts viewed on iPod or laptop by legions of fans with three-minute attention spans. For example, Rocketboom reports on world events to a daily audience of more than a hundred thousand, provocatively blurring newscast and spoof, employing a former MTV VJ as anchor. Attempts to cross over from the vlogosphere to film or television have been less successful, as the previous anchor of Rocketboom discovered upon being fired: She moved back home with her parents.

VOIP (NOUN OR ADJECTIVE)

Voice over Internet Protocol, the technical name for internet telephone service.

Sending spoken conversation by microphone over data networks typically used for email and web access, VoIP is often free but seldom reliable: it's jittery and vulnerable to blackout. Nevertheless, because price matters more than quality, and novelty reigns supreme in the realm of technology, telephone companies including Verizon and AT&T have entered the VoIP market, conveniently planning their own obsolescence.

WALLPAPER (NOUN OR VERB)

Screen decoration for PCs and cell phones.

Wallpaper is meant to personalize electronics in much the way that family photos are intended to humanize a cubicle, bringing a vision of outside life to the sterile digital environment. Vacation snapshots of sun-struck vistas, captured with a digital camera and uploaded onto the cell phone screen, are perennially popular, as are cuddly pics of pets. For those who spend their lives online, on the other hand, the wallpaper of choice, available on the web for a couple of dollars, tends to reflect favorite web-based escapes, including anime and, of course, pornography.

WAREZ (NOUN)

pronounced *wares*

Hacker slang for illegally copied and distributed software, often downloaded from P2P websites by the gigabyte.

The substitution of the letter z for s is a leetspeak mannerism—not unlike the tendency of teenage girls to dot their *i's* with hearts—which carries over into the various subcategories of warez: appz (software applications), gamez (computer games), MP3z (music in MP3 format), moviez (videos), and even bookz (digital books). While all warez break copyright law, crackz actually break into the software itself, to make duplication easier—and, of course, to taunt any copyright holder naive enough to think the free trade of warez can be limited.

WATERMARK (NOUN OR VERB)

A digital watermark adds information to an image, establishing copyright or authenticity, without noticeably altering the image itself.

Unlike traditional watermarks, which are pressed into wet paper during the process of manufacture, digital watermarks are usually added after the image is made, often by manipulating a few pixels in a busy area of the picture to encode the name of the copyright owner. Given that most photos are millions of pixels in size, the watermark will be seen only by those who know where to look.

WEB (NOUN)

The abbreviated name of the world wide web, also often shortened to *www*.

In Chinese, the web is called the *wan wei wang*, meaning "ten thousand-dimensional net," a rare understatement for a technology prone to phenomonal hype. Invented in 1990 by Tim Berners-Lee as a convenient way to share data at CERN (the European Organization for Nuclear Research), the web was worldwide only in name until scientists at the Stanford Linear Accelerator Center brought his software to the United States a year later. In short order, the web grew into an international research hub, beginning a trend that persists to this day: No matter how great the hype, the web surpasses it within six to eighteen months. With billion and billions of web pages in virtually all media, from text to video, the web is the world's foremost library. With billions and billions of dollars of business done online, the web is the world's foremost marketplace. Some say that it's alive. Some claim that it's the world's greatest intelligence. (Of course only the web knows the answer to such vastly complex questions.)

WHITE SPACE (NOUN)

A potentially lucrative market for which no products or services yet exist, because nobody has yet thought to make people desire those hypothetical products or services.

Once filled, white spaces starkly stand out as missed opportunities: Online auctions seem embarrassingly obvious post-eBay, and a web without wikis seems unthinkable now that Wikipedia dominates. As with inventions such as movable type, discerning the problem is often the greater feat than figuring out a specific solution. The dreamscape of high-tech entrepreneurs everywhere, white space is the Shangri-la of the internet.

WI-FI HOTSPOT (NOUN)

pronounced *why-fye hawt-spawt*

An area where the internet can be accessed wirelessly.

Wi-fi colloquially stands for "wireless fidelity," and a hotspot may be an individual apartment or whole metropolis. (Philadelphia plans to launch citywide internet access this year, with San Francisco soon to follow.) Wi-fi access standards, which are consistent worldwide, make such large-scale projects feasible, and also often make it possible for someone with a laptop to connect to private wi-fi hotspots while traveling. Leaving hotspots open for others to access freely is generally considered proper netiquette in the United States and Europe. In Singapore, though, connecting to a hotspot without permission is illegal—a crime nearly as serious as spitting on the street—potentially leading to a five-year prison sentence. As of this writing, there are no wi-fi hotspots in Singapore jails.

WIKI (NOUN)

pronounced *WICK-ee*

Derived from the Hawaiian word for "speedy," the term *wiki* refers to a quick-and-dirty means of collecting information from an online community, arranged on a website to which anyone can contribute new content or modify existing entries.

Any subject, from travel to genealogy, can spawn a wiki, though expansiveness comes naturally to this form of collaborative software, the information equivalent of a free-market economy. Like capitalism, the wiki can be spectacularly productive—with three million articles in every major language, Wikipedia.org covers exponentially more material than even the century-old *Britannica*—but also terribly divisive. In 2005, for instance, congressional staffers were caught anonymously vandalizing Wikipedia entries of political rivals. Wikis tend to handle such assaults in the same way that they filter out accidental misinformation: through an open-ended system of self-policing by users who value the collective good over their personal opinions.

WIKI U.

Is the traditional research university, built of brick and laced in ivy, technologically obsolete? Should Harvard and Yale and Columbia and Princeton all collectively be torn down in favor of a wiki?

Wikis are arguably more efficient than academia at doing what academia most values: reaching tentative consensus through broad collaboration. The concept of knowledge as a by-product of conversation worked well at Aristotle's lyceum and at the Royal Society in Newton's day, but in recent decades bureaucratic journals have fallen behind on publishing research, and underfunded departments have walled themselves off from outsiders. A scholarly wiki would compile research nearly instantaneously, at almost no cost, and hyperlinked entries on everything from Mayan calendar systems to quantum chromodynamics would make research truly interdisciplinary.

In the sciences at least, such ideas have been taken seriously. Futurist Kevin Kelly has worked out a rough structure for what he calls *wiki-science*, in which the hallowed system of peer review would be replaced with an ongoing process of collective revision of massively collaborative research papers. With over 1.5 million entries in English alone—and several million more in languages including German, French, Dutch, Polish, Japanese, and Russian—Wikipedia has demonstrated that such an approach can become stable and productive over several years. Moreover, the scientific journal *Nature* has reported that, even with amateurs writing and editing in their spare time, Wikipedia is nearly as accurate as the expertly produced *Encyclopædia Britannica* on scientific matters. Career academics fret about the lack of credentialing, forgetting that Aristotle lacked a PhD and even Einstein was once a patent office employee.

Efforts are also under way to put the wiki to work as a new kind of educational institution. A wikiversity would have a collaborative curriculum, and students would by and large be self-taught. There wouldn't be any fraternities or sororities—but perhaps a social networking site such as MySpace could serve as a virtual substitute.

WINDOW [NOUN]

Applications running on a PC are viewed through rectangular windows on the computer screen, framing word processing documents and web pages.

Windows are not exclusive to Microsoft Windows. In fact, back in 1989 Microsoft was sued by Apple, which had introduced windows to the Macintosh in 1984. The judge was unimpressed with Apple's case. Having been used in architecture for more than three thousand years, windows applied to computing are no great innovation. On the contrary, their very familiarity is what makes them such an apt metaphor.

WORD PROCESSOR (NOUN)

Software **for writing and editing text on a computer.**

The term *word processing* predates the actual phenomenon, in any practical sense, by a decade, originating as IBM marketing jargon for souped-up '60s-era typewriters. Nevertheless, even the idea that words might be processed without human intervention was enough to bring secretaries to the brink of revolt. With more than five hundred million copies of Microsoft Word now in use and secretaries nearly extinct, concerns about technology-supplanted jobs appear to be merited, yet the processing of words still has considerable limits, falling far short of IBM's initial promise to transform "ideas into written communications." Without close supervision, a spell-checker will change zine into zone, blog into blob, and phish into hash, and a grammar-checker will make hash of almost everything else. With multiple fonts and tools for adjusting layout, word processors are useful for document preparation—like food processors, which won't come up with the recipe, but will save time in the kitchen of a skilled cook.

WORM (NOUN)

Infesting the internet with malicious intent, the worm is a computer program adept at self-replication on unprotected computers and self-reproduction by email.

Unlike viruses, which primarily harm the host computer, worms generally do their damage to the entire network, overwhelming it by sheer numbers: On January 28, 2004, for instance, the infamous Mydoom worm was responsible for sending one in five emails worldwide. Yet general mayhem is often only a side effect of a more pointed attack on a specific company, such as Microsoft, which may find its systems overwhelmed when millions of infected computers are directed simultaneously to contact its servers. Whether this is criminal sabotage, as the FBI insists, or legitimate protest, as many hackers would claim, the even more pervasive use of worms by spammers, who distribute their sales messages over networks of so-called *zombie computers*, is a practice that only ad agencies could admire.

ZINE (NOUN)

pronounced *zeen*

An amateur magazine, inexpensively produced to address a special interest such as Chia Pet cultivation or computer game hacking.

Printed on photocopiers and freely passed around, early zines were necessarily slapdash, drawing on, and contributing to, the lo-fi punk style of the '80s. Desktop publishing has long since streamlined production, and the web has facilitated distribution, yet zinesters take care to maintain a do-it-yourself aesthetic, favoring novelty fonts and cheap clipart, pieced together with overt irony, to emphasize their nonmainstream status. Only in this so-called dirt-style look do they distinguish themselves from blogs about Chia Pet cultivation and computer game hacking. Zines are blogs that seek to be known for not being known.